FamilyCircle®

Hometown COOKING

Volume 2

Meredith® Books

Family Circle® Hometown Cooking

Editor: Jan Miller
Contributing Editors: Lisa Kingsley, Tricia Laning, Mary Williams, Waterbury Publications, Inc.
Contributing Writer: Lisa Kingsley, Waterbury Publications, Inc.
Contributing Designer: Ken Carlson, Waterbury Publications, Inc.
Editorial Assistant: Sheri Cord
Book Production Manager: Mark Weaver
Imaging Center Operator: Patricia Savage
Contributing Copy Editor: Ali Cybulski
Contributing Proofreaders: Steph Boeding, Susan J. Kling, Adam Morris
Contributing Indexer: Elizabeth T. Parson

Meredith® Books

Editorial Director: John Riha
Managing Editor: Kathleen Armentrout
Deputy Editor: Jennifer Darling
Group Editor: Jan Miller
Copy Chief: Doug Kouma
Senior Copy Editors: Kevin Cox, Jennifer Speer Ramundt, Elizabeth Keest Sedrel
Assistant Copy Editor: Metta Cederdahl
Proofreader: Joleen Ross

Executive Director, Sales: Ken Zagor
Director, Operations: George A. Susral
Director, Production: Douglas M. Johnston
Business Director: Janice Croat

Vice President and General Manager, SIP: Jeff Myers

Family Circle® Magazine

Editor in Chief: Linda Fears
Creative Director: Karmen Lizzul
Food Director: Regina Ragone
Senior Food Editor: Julie Miltenberger
Associate Food Editor: Michael Tyrrell
Assistant Food Editor: Cindy Heller
Editorial Assistant: Katie Kemple
Test Kitchen Associate: Althea Needham

Meredith Publishing Group

President: Jack Griffin
Executive Vice President: Doug Olson
Vice President, Manufacturing: Bruce Heston
Vice President, Consumer Marketing: David Ball
Vice President, Corporate Sales: Michael Brownstein
Consumer Product Marketing Director: Steve Swanson
Consumer Product Marketing Manager: Wendy Merical
Business Manager: Darren Tollefson

Meredith Corporation

Chairman of the Board: William T. Kerr
President and Chief Executive Officer: Stephen M. Lacy

In Memoriam: E.T. Meredith III (1933–2003)

Pictured on the front cover:
Brownie-Walnut Pie (page 173)

Cover photography:
Photographer: Pete Krumhardt
Food Stylist: Charles Worthington
Prop Stylist: Sue Mitchell

The Caribbean Grill sandwich recipe from the 2004 Search for the Greatest Grilled Cheese Sandwich in America Contest funded by DuPont (TM) Teflon® (page 155)

Cajun Beef Southwestern Salad recipe from the 2007 National Beef Cook-Off® funded by the Beef Checkoff. www.beefcookoff.org (page 92)

Jumbo Shell Pasta Stuffed with Baby White Cheddar and Chicken Macaroni recipe from the 2007 Tillamook® Macaroni & Cheese Recipe Contest grand prize winner, Lorie Roach (page 133)

Enjoy prizewinning recipes from hometown America!

Home cooks who win recipe contests and cook-offs know what it's like to taste victory. It's probably what spurs them to spend hours in the kitchen, making and remaking a recipe until it's perfect—and to keep entering contest after contest. The collection of recipes in *Family Circle® Hometown Cooking Volume 2* celebrates that very American tradition—and brings some of the best of those prizewinning recipes from cooking competitions across the country into your kitchen. Among the more than 150 recipes are dishes for special breakfasts, last-minute weekday meals, potluck favorites to please any palate, and a yummy selection of everyone's favorite, desserts. Along the way, you'll meet some of the cooks who contributed recipes to this book—and learn a little about their recipes. When you taste them, you'll know why they were winners.

—the editors

Contents

Chapter 1

Getting Started

Start the party—and keep it going—with this selection of nibbles, noshes, and beverages both hot and cold. Fresh takes on reliable classics and a few bold, new ideas will please every palate.

Ancho Shrimp on Smoked Gouda Corncakes

Ancho Shrimp on Smoked Gouda Corncakes

Lori Stephens' first-place prize in the 2008 National Cornbread Cook-Off, sponsored by Lodge® Manufacturing and Martha White®, was $5,000 and a range donated by Brown Stove Works. "I gave the stove to my mother," Lori, of Hendersonville, Tennessee, says, "because she's such a fabulous cook and because she taught everyone in our family to cook."

PREP: 20 minutes
COOK: about 25 minutes
MAKES: 8 appetizer servings

Smoked Gouda Corncakes:
- 1 **tablespoon butter**
- 1 **cup fresh or frozen whole kernel corn**
- ⅓ **cup sliced scallions**
- 1 **egg**
- 1⅓ **cups Martha White® Yellow Self-Rising Cornmeal Mix**
- 1 **cup buttermilk**
- 3 **tablespoons sour cream**
- 1½ **cups shredded smoked Gouda cheese (6 ounces)**
- ¼ to ½ **cup Crisco® canola oil**

Ancho Shrimp:
- ¼ **cup (½ stick) butter**
- 2 **large dried ancho chiles, split in half and seeds removed**
- 1 **tablespoon minced garlic**
- 1 **pound fresh shrimp, peeled and deveined**
  Salt and black pepper
- 1 **cup undrained canned petite diced tomatoes**
  Sliced scallions, for serving

1. Smoked Gouda Corncakes: In 10-inch Lodge® cast-iron skillet, melt 1 tablespoon butter over medium heat. Add corn and ⅓ cup scallions. Cook for 2 minutes. In large bowl, lightly beat egg. Add cornmeal mix, buttermilk and sour cream; whisk until smooth. Stir in cheese and corn-scallion mixture. Wipe out skillet with a paper towel. Add 2 tablespoons of the canola oil to skillet; heat over medium-high heat. Spoon batter into pan by scant ¼ cupfuls and spread to about 3-inch rounds. Cook for 3 to 4 minutes or until golden brown, turning once. If corncakes brown too quickly, reduce heat to medium. Cook 3 or 4 at a time, adding more oil as needed. Drain on paper towels. Wipe out skillet.

2. Ancho Shrimp: Melt ¼ cup butter in skillet over medium-high heat. Add ancho chiles; cook for 3 minutes. Add garlic; cook for 1 minute. Add shrimp; sprinkle with salt and pepper. Cook until shrimp turn pink, stirring occasionally. Stir in tomatoes; cook just until hot. Remove and discard ancho chiles.

3. To serve, place 2 corncakes, slightly overlapping, on each serving plate. Top with ancho shrimp. Sprinkle with additional scallions.

Per serving: 387 cal., 24 g total fat (10 g sat. fat), 138 mg chol., 724 mg sodium, 26 g carbo., 4 g fiber, 19 g pro.

Asparagus and Walnut Puffs

When breast cancer survivor Carole Resnick's recipe was named a prizewinner in the 2008 I Love Walnuts! recipe contest sponsored by the California Walnut Board, she gave the prize—a Kitchen-Aid stand mixer—to a breast cancer support group in her hometown of Cleveland, Ohio, to be auctioned off at a fundraiser. Winning, she says, "just makes me feel good."

PREP: 20 minutes
BAKE: at 375° for 22 to 25 minutes
MAKES: 6 appetizer servings

 1 **frozen puff pastry sheet (½ of a 17.3-ounce package), thawed**
 1 **cup ricotta cheese**
 1 **cup finely shredded Parmesan cheese (4 ounces)**
 ¾ **cup finely chopped California English walnuts**
 2 **tablespoons chopped fresh basil leaves**
 ¼ **to ½ teaspoon salt**
 ¼ **teaspoon freshly ground black pepper**
 12 **to 18 asparagus spears, trimmed and cleaned**
 1 **tablespoon walnut oil**

1. Heat oven to 375°. Line large baking sheet with parchment paper or a silicone baking mat.

2. Roll pastry into a 12×9-inch rectangle, about ¼ inch thick. Cut into six 4×3-inch rectangles. Place rectangles on prepared baking sheet; set aside.

3. In medium-size bowl, combine ricotta cheese, Parmesan cheese, walnuts, basil, salt and pepper. Mix well. Spread ⅙ of the walnut mixture on each pastry rectangle, leaving a ½-inch border on each side.

4. In another medium-size bowl, toss asparagus spears with walnut oil. Place 2 to 3 asparagus spears on each pastry rectangle. Bake at 375° for 22 to 25 minutes or until pastry is puffed and golden and asparagus is tender. Serve immediately.

Per serving: 474 cal., 36 g total fat (11 g sat. fat), 30 mg chol., 460 mg sodium, 23 g carbo., 2 g fiber, 16 g pro.

Asparagus and Walnut Puffs

Asian Chicken Wings

These tasty wings are cooked in a sweet-spicy concoction of soy sauce, ginger, leek, garlic, five-spice powder, and chiles. Serve them hot or cold—with teriyaki sauce, or not.

PREP: 25 minutes
COOK: 20 to 25 minutes
MAKES: 12 to 18 appetizers

 2 to 3 pounds chicken wings (12 to 18 wings)
 1½ cups water
 ⅔ cup soy sauce
 1 leek, washed and finely chopped*
 4 slices fresh ginger
 1 tablespoon sugar
 1 tablespoon vinegar
 2 or 3 dried red chiles
 ½ teaspoon purchased five-spice powder or Homemade Five-Spice Powder (see recipe, right)
 2 cloves garlic, minced
 Bottled teriyaki sauce (optional)

1. Cut off and discard tips of chicken wings. Cut wings at joints, if desired, to form 24 to 36 pieces.

2. In 4-quart Dutch oven, combine water, soy sauce, leek, ginger, sugar, vinegar, chiles, five-spice powder and garlic. Bring to a boil. Add chicken. Return to a boil; reduce heat. Cover and simmer for 20 to 25 minutes or until chicken is no longer pink.

3. Remove chicken wings with slotted spoon. Place wings in a serving dish. If desired, brush with teriyaki sauce and serve with additional teriyaki sauce for dipping. (Or, chill wings in the refrigerator for 4 to 12 hours. If desired, serve cold wings with additional teriyaki sauce for dipping.)

*Note: To wash leeks, slice them, then swish in cool water; spin dry in a salad spinner or drain in a colander and pat dry with paper towels.

Per appetizer: 123 cal., 9 g total fat (2 g sat. fat), 58 mg chol., 204 mg sodium, 0 g carbo., 0 g fiber, 10 g pro.

Homemade Five-Spice Powder: In a small bowl, combine 1 teaspoon ground cinnamon; 1 teaspoon anise seed, crushed; ¼ teaspoon fennel seed, crushed; ¼ teaspoon Szechuan pepper, crushed; and ⅛ teaspoon ground cloves. Store extra in a covered container up to 1 month. Makes about 1 tablespoon.

Supreme Pizza Fondue

This fun appetizer is a bit like deconstructed pizza. All of the elements are there—sausage, sauce, mushrooms, veggies, plus bread and cheese cubes for dipping.

PREP: 20 minutes
COOK: 15 minutes
MAKES: 4 cups (16 servings)

- ¼ pound bulk Italian sausage
- 1 small onion, finely chopped (⅓ cup)
- 1 clove garlic, minced
- 1 jar (26 ounces) tomato pasta sauce
- 1 cup chopped fresh mushrooms
- ⅔ cup chopped pepperoni or Canadian-style bacon
- 1 teaspoon dried basil or oregano
- ½ cup chopped pitted ripe olives (optional)
- ¼ cup finely chopped green pepper (optional)
  Italian flat bread (focaccia) or Italian bread cubes, cooked tortellini or mozzarella or provolone cheese cubes, for serving

1. In large skillet, cook sausage, onion and garlic over medium heat until meat is brown. Drain off fat.

2. Add pasta sauce, mushrooms, pepperoni and basil. Bring to a boil; reduce heat. Cover and simmer for 10 minutes. If desired, stir in ripe olives and green pepper. Cover and cook for 5 minutes more or until pepper is tender. Serve with bread cubes, tortellini and cheese cubes for dipping.

Per ¼ cup fondue: 80 cal., 5 g total fat (2 g sat. fat), 11 mg chol., 361 mg sodium, 7 g carbo., 1 g fiber, 3 g pro.

Slow Cooker Directions: Prepare as above through Step 1, except in 3½- or 4-quart slow cooker combine pasta sauce, mushrooms, pepperoni and basil. Stir in the sausage mixture. Cover slow cooker; cook on low-heat setting for 3 hours. If desired, stir in ripe olives and green pepper. Cover; cook on low-heat setting for 15 minutes more. Serve as above.

Spicy Slow Cooked Seafood Dip

This elegant dip couldn't be easier to make: Toss a few ingredients in the slow cooker, turn it on, then turn your attention to the rest of the party.

PREP: 25 minutes
COOK: 1½ hours on high-heat setting
MAKES: 16 to 20 servings

- 1 medium-size sweet red pepper, finely chopped (¾ cup)
- 1 medium-size jalapeño chile, finely chopped (optional)
- 1 medium-size onion, finely chopped (½ cup)
- 4 cups shredded Monterey Jack cheese with jalapeño chiles (1 pound)
- ⅔ cup mayonnaise
- 2 packages (6 ounces each) refrigerated crab claw meat, drained
- 7 to 8 ounces peeled and deveined cooked baby shrimp
- ½ cup heavy cream
- 2 tablespoons all-purpose flour
- 1 teaspoon paprika
  Sliced chiles
  Crostini*, sliced vegetables and/or breadsticks, for serving

1. In 3½- or 4-quart slow cooker, combine sweet pepper, jalapeño chile (if desired), onion, cheese, mayonnaise, crab, shrimp, heavy cream, flour and paprika; mix well.

2. Cover slow cooker; cook on high-heat setting for 1½ hours or until melted and bubbly. Keep warm on the warm or low-heat setting, or transfer to a chafing dish and hold for up to 2 hours. Garnish with sliced chiles. Serve with crostini, vegetables and/or breadsticks.

*Note: To make crostini, heat oven to 425°. Cut a baguette lengthwise into thin slices. Brush lightly with 3 tablespoons olive oil. Place in a single layer on very large baking sheet. Bake at 425° for 12 to 15 minutes or until lightly browned, turning once.

Per serving (no dippers): 241 cal., 20 g total fat (9 g sat. fat), 95 mg chol., 358 mg sodium, 2 g carbo., 0 g fiber, 14 g pro.

Bacon and Cheese Stuffed Dates

A savory filling of soft, melty warm cheese flavored with bacon, scallions and garlic makes these sweet dates irresistible. They will disappear the minute they appear from the oven.

PREP: 25 minutes
BAKE: at 350° for 5 to 8 minutes
MAKES: 24 stuffed dates

  2 **strips bacon, crisp-cooked, drained and finely crumbled or ¼ cup chopped prosciutto (about 2 ounces)**
  ¼ **cup thinly sliced scallions (2)**
  2 **cloves garlic, minced**
  1 **package (3 ounces) cream cheese, softened**
  ½ **cup Cambozola cheese or crumbled blue cheese (about 2 ounces)**
  2 **teaspoons Dijon mustard**
  ⅛ **teaspoon black pepper**
 24 **Medjool dates (about 16 ounces unpitted)**

1. Heat oven to 350°. In medium-size bowl, stir together bacon, scallions and garlic. Add cream cheese, Cambozola, mustard and pepper. Stir to combine.

2. Make a lengthwise slit in each date with a knife. Spread each date open slightly. Remove pits. Fill each date with a rounded teaspoon of the bacon mixture. Place dates, filling side up, on baking sheet. Bake at 350° for 5 to 8 minutes or until heated. Serve warm.

Make-Ahead Directions: Stuff dates, cover and refrigerate up to 24 hours. Uncover and bake as directed just before serving.

Per stuffed date: 92 cal., 2 g total fat (1 g sat. fat), 6 mg chol., 69 mg sodium, 18 g carbo., 2 g fiber, 1 g pro.

Party Nachos

Sure, these are perfect for a party, but they make a fun casual supper, too. If you want to add a little more nutrition to the dish, scatter some diced cooked chicken on top before baking—and sprinkle with shredded lettuce and sliced radishes before serving.

PREP: 10 minutes
BAKE: at 400° for 5 to 7 minutes per batch
MAKES: 8 to 10 servings

    8 ounces tortilla chips (about 10 cups)
    2 cups shredded Cheddar cheese (8 ounces)
    2 cups shredded Monterey Jack cheese (8 ounces)
    3 scallions, sliced
    1 cup chopped seeded tomato
    1 can (4 ounces) diced green chiles, drained
    1 can (2¼ ounces) sliced pitted ripe olives, drained
    1 can (15 ounces) black beans, rinsed and drained
       Purchased salsa, sour cream and/or purchased
       guacamole (optional), for serving

1. Heat oven to 400°. Divide tortilla chips between two 12-inch round pizza pans. Top chips with half of the Cheddar cheese, half of the Monterey Jack cheese, the scallions, tomato and chiles. Sprinkle with remaining cheeses, the olives and black beans.

2. Bake, one pan at a time, at 400° for 5 to 7 minutes or until cheese melts. Serve immediately. If desired, serve with salsa, sour cream and/or guacamole.

Per serving: 414 cal., 27 g total fat (13 g sat. fat), 55 mg chol., 720 mg sodium, 28 g carbo., 5 g fiber, 20 g pro.

Hot Artichoke Spread

Is there anyone who doesn't love this fabulously rich, velvety hot dip? This version makes use of light ingredients—cream cheese, mayonnaise, and sour cream—so you can enjoy more of it with less guilt. Try one of the tasty variations, too.

PREP: 30 minutes
BAKE: at 350° for 30 to 35 minutes
MAKES: about 5 cups

- ¾ cup finely chopped onion
- 2 cloves garlic, minced
- 1 tablespoon butter
- 2 packages (8 ounces each) reduced-fat cream cheese (Neufchâtel), softened
- 1½ cups grated Parmesan cheese
- ¼ cup milk
- ¼ cup light mayonnaise
- ¼ cup light sour cream
- ¼ teaspoon freshly ground black pepper
- 3 cups chopped fresh spinach leaves
- 1 can (14 ounces) artichoke hearts, drained and chopped
  Bagel chips or sliced French bread, for serving

1. Heat oven to 350°. In medium-size skillet, cook onion and garlic in hot butter over medium heat for 3 to 4 minutes or until tender. Set aside to cool.

2. In large bowl, stir together cream cheese, Parmesan cheese, milk, mayonnaise, sour cream and pepper. Stir in spinach, artichoke hearts and onion mixture. Spread mixture into a 10-inch quiche dish or deep-dish pie plate, or use 2 smaller au gratin dishes.

3. Bake at 350° for 30 to 35 minutes (20 to 25 minutes if using au gratin dishes) or until heated through and beginning to brown. Serve with bagel chips or sliced French bread.

Make-Ahead Directions: Prepare as directed through Step 2. Cover and refrigerate up to 24 hours. Heat oven to 350°. Uncover and bake at 350° about 40 minutes for the quiche dish (or about 25 minutes for the au gratin dishes) or until bubbly.

Per tablespoon spread: 29 cal., 2 g total fat (1 g sat. fat), 7 mg chol., 68 mg sodium, 1 g carbo., 0 g fiber, 1 g pro.

Hot Sausage and Mushroom Spread: Prepare as directed in Step 1, except omit the butter and cook ½ pound bulk hot Italian sausage, 2 cups sliced fresh mushrooms and ½ cup chopped green or sweet red pepper with the onion and garlic; drain off fat. Set sausage mixture aside to cool. For Step 2, substitute 1 cup shredded mozzarella cheese for 1 cup of the Parmesan cheese and omit the artichoke hearts.

Hot Feta Cheese and Olive Spread: Prepare as directed in Step 1. For Step 2, substitute 1 cup crumbled feta cheese with basil and tomato for 1 cup of the Parmesan cheese; substitute ½ cup halved, pitted kalamata olives for the artichokes; and stir 2 tablespoons chopped fresh basil in with the spinach and onion mixture. Continue with Step 3. If desired, serve with toasted soft pita wedges.*

***Note:** To toast pita wedges, heat oven 350°. Split 8 large pita bread rounds in half horizontally. If desired, lightly coat the cut side of each pita bread half with non-stick cooking spray; sprinkle lightly with cracked black pepper. Cut each half into 6 wedges (96 wedges total). Spread wedges in a single layer on large baking sheets (you will need to bake chips in batches). Bake at 350° for 10 to 12 minutes or until crisp.

Sweet and Sassy Meatballs

The smaller scale of the meatballs used in this dish (at 32 per pound, they're about half of an ounce each) makes them better suited to being party fare. They can easily be eaten in a bite or two with a toothpick or cocktail fork.

PREP: 10 minutes
COOK: 10 minutes
MAKES: 64 meatballs

- 1 can (16 ounces) jellied cranberry sauce
- 1 bottle (18 ounces) barbecue sauce
- 2 packages (1 pound each) frozen cooked meatballs, thawed (32 per pound)

1. In large skillet, stir together cranberry sauce and barbecue sauce. Cook over medium heat until cranberry sauce is melted, stirring occasionally.

2. Add meatballs to sauce mixture. Cook, uncovered, about 10 minutes or until meatballs are heated through, stirring occasionally. To serve, keep warm in a chafing dish or slow cooker.

Make-Ahead Directions: Prepare as directed in Step 1. Stir in frozen or thawed meatballs. Cover and refrigerate up to 24 hours. In large skillet, heat meatballs and sauce over medium heat until heated through, stirring occasionally.

Per 4 meatballs: 60 cal., 4 g total fat (2 g sat. fat), 5 mg chol., 177 mg sodium, 5 g carbo., 1 g fiber, 2 g pro.

Meatballs in Chipotle Sauce: Prepare as directed, except substitute 1 bottle (12 ounces) chili sauce for the barbecue sauce and stir in 3 to 4 tablespoons finely chopped canned chipotle chiles in adobo sauce.

Meatballs in Hawaiian Sauce: Prepare as directed, except substitute 1 can (8 ounces) crushed pineapple for the cranberry sauce.

Chili Mixed Nuts

Perfect for munching and watching the big game—or simply as a pre-dinner party nibble—these chili-lime nuts are super-simple to make and can be frozen for up to 3 months to have at the ready. Use your favorite nut or a blend.

PREP: 10 minutes
BAKE: at 325° for 15 minutes
MAKES: 3 cups

- 2 **tablespoons (¼ stick) butter, melted**
- 1 **tablespoon chili powder**
- 1 **tablespoon lime juice**
- 1 **teaspoon garlic salt**
- 3 **cups mixed nuts or peanuts**

1. Heat oven to 325°. In small bowl, combine melted butter, chili powder, lime juice and garlic salt. In 15×10×1-inch baking pan, combine butter mixture and nuts. Toss to coat evenly.

2. Bake at 325° for 15 minutes, stirring twice. Spread nuts on a large piece of foil to cool. Store in an airtight container at room temperature up to 2 weeks or freeze up to 3 months.

Per ¼ cup: 223 cal., 20 g total fat (4 g sat. fat), 5 mg chol., 104 mg sodium, 9 g carbo., 3 g fiber, 6 g pro.

Creamy Dill Dip

This yummy chip-and-veggie dip is two dips in one. Flavor it with delicate, aromatic dill—or with Parmesan cheese and Italian seasoning.

PREP: 10 minutes
CHILL: 1 hour
MAKES: about 2 cups

- 1 package (8 ounces) cream cheese, softened
- 1 carton (8 ounces) sour cream
- 2 tablespoons finely chopped scallion
- 2 tablespoons chopped fresh dill or 2 teaspoons dried dill
- ½ teaspoon seasoned salt or salt
  Milk (optional)
  Assorted vegetable dippers, crackers or chips, for serving

1. In medium-size mixing bowl, beat cream cheese, sour cream, scallion, dill and salt with electric mixer on low speed until fluffy. Cover and refrigerate at least 1 hour or up to 24 hours. If dip is too thick after chilling, stir in 1 to 2 tablespoons milk. Serve with vegetable dippers, crackers and/or chips.

Per tablespoon dip: 40 cal., 4 g total fat (2 g sat. fat), 11 mg chol., 49 mg sodium, 1 g carbo., 0 g fiber, 1 g pro.

Creamy Parmesan Dip: Prepare Creamy Dill Dip as directed, except omit dill and salt. Stir ⅓ cup grated Parmesan cheese and 2 teaspoons dried Italian seasoning into the beaten cream cheese mixture.

Double-Quick Shrimp Cocktail

Two sauces served in the same bowl makes for a great presentation. Start by pouring half of one sauce on one side of the bowl, then half of the other sauce on the other side—then add the remainder of each sauce. They will meet in the middle but won't run together. If this makes you nervous, just serve the sauces in two separate bowls—they still taste great.

PREP: 15 minutes
CHILL: up to 4 hours
MAKES: about 40 servings

- 1 carton (8 ounces) sour cream
- ¼ cup prepared horseradish
- 2 tablespoons chopped fresh chives or thinly sliced scallion tops
- 1 tablespoon lemon juice
- 1 jar (12 ounces) seafood cocktail sauce or chili sauce
- 1½ pounds (60 to 75) frozen peeled and cooked shrimp with tails, thawed
  Fresh chives and/or lemon slices or wedges, for garnish

1. In small bowl, combine sour cream, horseradish, 2 tablespoons chives and lemon juice. Place half of the sour cream mixture in one side of a 4-cup shallow serving bowl. Spoon half of the cocktail sauce into bowl next to sour cream mixture. Spoon the rest of the sour cream mixture over the sour cream mixture in bowl and the rest of the cocktail sauce over the cocktail sauce in bowl. If desired, cover and refrigerate up to 4 hours before serving.

2. To serve, place bowl containing dip mixture on a platter. Arrange shrimp around bowl. Garnish with chives and/or lemon slices or wedges.

Per serving: 37 cal., 1 g total fat (1 g sat. fat), 36 mg chol., 119 mg sodium, 2 g carbo., 0 g fiber, 4 g pro.

Ginger Peach Freeze

Add spark to the start of a summer party with this refreshing fruit ice. It whets the appetite but is so light, it won't spoil your supper.

PREP: 10 minutes
STAND: 30 minutes
FREEZE: 3 hours
MAKES: 8 servings

- 1 cup water
- 1 cup sugar
- 3 tablespoons lemon juice
- ¼ teaspoon ground ginger
- 1 package (16 ounces) frozen unsweetened peach slices
  Fresh peach slices (optional)

1. In medium-size saucepan, combine water, sugar, lemon juice and ginger. Bring to a boil. Remove from heat; add frozen peaches. Let stand about 30 minutes or until peaches are thawed and mixture has cooled.

2. Place half of the peach mixture in a blender. Cover and blend until smooth. Transfer blended mixture to 12×8×2-inch baking dish. Place remaining peach mixture in blender. Cover and blend until smooth; add to the baking dish.

3. Cover and freeze for 3 to 4 hours. Break up mixture with a fork; spoon into dessert dishes. If desired, top with fresh peach slices.

Per ½ cup serving: 119 cal., 0 g total fat (0 g sat. fat), 0 mg chol., 1 mg sodium, 31 g carbo., 1 g fiber, 0 g pro.

Lime-Tea Punch

Bottled blends of black tea and fruit juices are all the rage. This fresh punch takes off on that trend. Use a medium-grade black tea, such as an orange pekoe.

PREP: 10 minutes
COOL: 15 minutes
CHILL: 4 to 24 hours
MAKES: 16 servings

- 8 **individual-size black tea bags**
- 6 **cups boiling water**
- 2 **tablespoons honey**
- 1 **can (12 ounces) frozen limeade concentrate**
- 4 **cups ginger ale, chilled**
  Ice cubes
- 1 **lime, cut into wedges, for garnish**

1. Steep tea bags in the boiling water for 5 minutes; remove tea bags and discard. Cool for 15 minutes. Stir in honey until dissolved. Stir in limeade concentrate until melted. Cover and refrigerate mixture for at least 4 hours or up to 24 hours.

2. To serve, transfer tea mixture to a punch bowl; add ginger ale and ice cubes. Garnish with lime wedges.

Make-Ahead Directions: Prepare tea mixture as directed in Step 1; cover and chill for up to 48 hours.

Per ⅔-cup serving: 73 cal., 0 g total fat (0 g sat. fat), 0 mg chol., 9 mg sodium, 19 g carbo., 0 g fiber, 0 g pro.

Hot Orange and Mocha Drink

Here's the perfect way to keep warm on a cold winter night: Curl up in front of the fire with this citrus-and-cinnamon-spiked mocha drink and a good book.

PREP: 15 minutes
COOK: 5 minutes
MAKES: 6 servings

- 1 **orange**
- 5 **cups hot strong coffee**
- ½ **cup unsweetened cocoa powder**
- ½ **cup packed brown sugar**
- ¼ **teaspoon ground cinnamon**
- ½ **cup heavy cream, half-and-half or light cream**

Whipped Honey-Orange Topping:
- ½ **cup heavy cream**
- 1 **tablespoon honey**
- 1 **tablespoon orange liqueur or orange juice (optional)**
   Orange peel curls (optional)*, for serving

1. Remove the peel from the orange in strips with a vegetable peeler, being careful not to remove the white pith. In large saucepan, combine the peel and hot coffee. Cook over medium-low heat for 5 minutes. Remove the peel with a slotted spoon and discard.

2. In small bowl, whisk together cocoa powder, brown sugar and cinnamon. Whisk cocoa mixture into hot coffee until well combined. Stir in ½ cup heavy cream.

3. Whipped Honey-Orange Topping: In chilled small bowl, combine ½ cup heavy cream, honey and, if desired, orange liqueur or juice. Beat with chilled beaters of an electric mixer on low speed or beat with a whisk until soft peaks form.

4. If desired, froth the coffee mixture with an immersion blender. To serve, ladle coffee mixture into 6 coffee mugs. Top each serving with a spoonful of Whipped Honey-Orange Topping. If desired, garnish with orange peel curls.

Icy Orange and Mocha Drink: Prepare as at left, except cover and refrigerate coffee mixture up to 3 days. Serve chilled in tall glasses over ice.

*Note: To make orange peel curls, remove long thin strips of peel from orange with a vegetable peeler. Wrap the strips around wooden skewers and let stand for several minutes.

Per about 7-ounce serving: 256 cal., 17 g total fat (9 g sat. fat), 55 mg chol., 24 mg sodium, 25 g carbo., 0 g fiber, 3 g pro.

Hot Spiced Cider

This fall classic perfumes the whole house with its warm, spicy scent as it simmers. It works equally well with either cider or juice.

PREP: 10 minutes
COOK: 15 minutes
MAKES: 8 servings

- 8 **cups apple cider or apple juice**
- ¼ **cup packed brown sugar**
- 6 **inches stick cinnamon**
- 1 **teaspoon whole allspice**
- 1 **teaspoon whole cloves**
- 1 **teaspoon shredded orange peel**
- 8 **thin orange wedges (optional)**
- 8 **whole cloves (optional)**

1. In large saucepan, combine cider and brown sugar. For spice bag, place cinnamon, allspice, the 1 teaspoon cloves and orange peel in center of a double-thick, 6-inch square of 100-percent cotton cheesecloth. Bring corners of the cheesecloth together and tie with a clean kitchen string. Add spice bag to the saucepan with cider mixture.

2. Bring mixture to a boil; reduce heat. Cover and simmer for 10 minutes. If desired, stud orange wedges with cloves.

3. To serve, remove spice bag and discard. Serve cider in mugs. If desired, garnish with studded orange wedges.

Per 8-ounce serving: 122 cal., 0 g total fat (0 g sat. fat), 0 mg chol., 9 mg sodium, 31 g carbo., 1 g fiber, 0 g pro.

Chapter 2

Bring On Breakfast

Wake up to some great ideas for your next weekend morning or holiday brunch. A savory hot egg dish, bread or refreshing fruit salad is a beautiful way to start—or celebrate—the day.

Mediterranean Frittata

Lemon Buttermilk Ricotta Pancakes
with Berries and Sweet Lemon Sauce

Lemon Buttermilk Ricotta Pancakes with Berries and Sweet Lemon Sauce

Joanne Nichols' fruit-filled pancakes garnered the innkeeper of the Arbor Inn in Rye, New Hampshire, first place in BedandBreakfast.com's 2008 "Pancakes with Personality" contest. She won $1,000 plus $2,000 worth of bed-and-breakfast stays throughout the country—where she will no doubt be checking on the competition in the friendliest way.

PREP: 25 minutes
STAND: 10 to 15 minutes
COOK: 2 to 4 minutes per batch
MAKES: approximately 16 pancakes

Pancakes:

- 1½ **cups unbleached all-purpose flour**
- 2 **tablespoons granulated sugar**
- 1 **teaspoon baking powder**
- ½ **teaspoon baking soda**
- ½ **teaspoon salt**
- 2 **eggs, separated**
- 1¼ **cups buttermilk**
- ½ **cup ricotta cheese**
- ¼ **cup orange juice**
- 2 **tablespoons vegetable oil**
- 1 **teaspoon lemon extract**
- 1 **tablespoon finely shredded lemon peel**
  Butter, for cooking pancakes
- 2 **cups assorted fresh berries, such as blueberries, raspberries, blackberries and sliced strawberries**

Sweet Lemon Sauce:

- 1 **cup sugar**
- ½ **cup (1 stick) butter**
- ¼ **cup water**
- 1 **egg yolk**
- 1 **tablespoon finely shredded lemon peel**
- 3 **tablespoons lemon juice**
  Additional berries and/or lemon wedges, for serving

1. Pancakes: In medium-size bowl, mix flour, 2 tablespoons sugar, baking powder, baking soda and salt. Make a well in center of flour mixture; set aside.

2. In another medium-size bowl, combine 2 egg yolks, buttermilk, ricotta, orange juice, oil and lemon extract. Whisk until smooth. Add yolk mixture to flour mixture; stir just until moistened. Batter should be slightly lumpy.

3. Sprinkle 1 tablespoon lemon peel over top of batter. In small mixing bowl, beat egg whites with an electric mixer on high speed until stiff. Fold whites into batter just until incorporated. Let stand 10 to 15 minutes.

4. Sweet Lemon Sauce: In medium-size stainless steel saucepan, combine 1 cup sugar, ½ cup butter, water, 1 egg yolk, 1 tablespoon lemon peel and lemon juice. Cook and stir over medium heat until butter melts and sugar dissolves. Bring to a boil; reduce heat. Simmer, uncovered, for 1 to 2 minutes. Remove from heat; keep warm.

5. Melt a little butter in large skillet over medium-low heat. Pour ¼ cup batter per pancake onto skillet. When pancakes have risen slightly, place berries on top, pressing lightly. When bottoms begin to brown and surface is bubbly, turn and cook until lightly browned.

6. Arrange pancakes on a platter. Garnish with berries and lemon wedges. Serve with lemon sauce and butter.

Per pancake with 1 tablespoon sauce: 217 cal., 10 g total fat (5 g sat. fat), 61 mg chol., 217 mg sodium, 28 g carbo., 1 g fiber, 4 g pro.

Sausage, Pepper and Cheese Quiche with Corn Bread Crust

After only his second try, Earl Bandy Jr. of Knoxville, Tennessee, has cooking contest fever. His Southwestern-style brunch dish won third prize in the 2008 National Cornbread Cook-Off. "We took about 30 people down there with us and just had a blast," he says. He came home with two very large Lodge® cast-iron pans—and inspiration for the following year.

PREP: 25 minutes
BAKE: 10 to 12 minutes at 400° plus 40 minutes at 350°
COOL: 5 minutes
MAKES: 8 servings

Corn Bread Crust:
- 2 tablespoons Crisco® vegetable oil
- ½ teaspoon baking soda
- ¾ cup buttermilk
- 1 can (15¼ ounces) whole kernel corn, drained
- 1 cup Martha White® cornmeal
- 1 can (4 ounces) diced green chiles, drained
- 1 egg, lightly beaten
- ½ teaspoon salt

Filling:
- 5 eggs, lightly beaten
- 1 cup half-and-half or light cream
- 1 teaspoon ground cumin
- ½ teaspoon salt
- ½ teaspoon black pepper
- 1 pound hot bulk pork sausage, cooked and drained
- 1 cup chopped green and/or sweet red peppers
- 1 cup sliced fresh mushrooms
- ½ cup chopped scallions (4)
- 1½ cups shredded yellow and/or white Cheddar cheese (6 ounces)
  Sour cream, sliced cherry tomatoes, sliced avocado and chopped fresh cilantro leaves, for serving (optional)

1. Corn Bread Crust: Heat oven to 400°. Pour oil into a 12-inch Lodge® cast-iron skillet, tilting to coat the bottom; place in oven for 7 to 8 minutes or until hot.

2. While skillet is heating, stir baking soda into buttermilk; let stand for 5 minutes. In large bowl, combine buttermilk mixture, corn, cornmeal, chiles, 1 egg and ½ teaspoon salt. Stir until well mixed. Pour into hot skillet. Bake at 400° for 10 to 12 minutes or until lightly browned.

3. Filling: Reduce oven temperature to 350°. In large bowl, with wire whisk or rotary beater, beat together 5 eggs, half-and-half, cumin, ½ teaspoon salt and black pepper. Layer sausage, green peppers, mushrooms, scallions, and cheese over crust. Pour egg mixture over the top.

4. Bake quiche at 350° for 40 to 45 minutes or until golden brown and set. Cool for 5 minutes before serving. Cut into wedges. If desired, serve with sour cream, cherry tomatoes, avocado and cilantro.

Per serving: 525 cal., 36 g total fat (15 g sat. fat), 236 mg chol., 1,163 mg sodium, 28 g carbo., 3 g fiber, 23 g pro.

Sausage, Pepper and Cheese
Quiche with Corn Bread Crust

Stuffed Croissant French Toast

Croissants get the French toast treatment. Elegant and completely indulgent, these cream cheese and fresh strawberry-stuffed pastries make an impressive Valentine's Day or Mother's Day breakfast in bed.

PREP: 25 minutes
COOK: 2 to 4 minutes per batch
MAKES: 4 stuffed croissants

- 1 package (8 ounces) cream cheese, softened
- ¼ cup pure maple syrup or maple-flavored syrup
- ½ cup chopped fresh strawberries
- 4 large croissants
- 2 eggs
- ½ cup half-and-half or light cream
- 1 tablespoon packed brown sugar
- ½ teaspoon ground cinnamon
- ½ teaspoon ground nutmeg
- Halved fresh strawberries, for serving
- Pure maple syrup or maple-flavored syrup, for serving

1. In medium-size mixing bowl, beat cream cheese and ¼ cup maple syrup with electric mixer on medium speed until well combined. Stir in ½ cup chopped strawberries. With serrated knife, carefully cut each croissant in half horizontally, leaving one side intact. Spoon cream cheese filling into each croissant.

2. In large bowl, with wire whisk or rotary beater, beat together eggs, half-and-half, brown sugar, cinnamon and nutmeg. Using your hands, carefully dip each side of filled croissants in the egg mixture, being careful not to squeeze out filling. Cook filled croissants, two at a time if necessary, on lightly greased extra-large skillet or griddle over medium heat for 1 to 2 minutes on each side or until golden brown. If necessary, use a spatula and a fork to turn croissants. Some filling may leak out onto the griddle. If necessary, wipe off griddle and lightly grease again before cooking remaining croissants.

3. Serve warm, topped with halved strawberries and drizzled with additional maple syrup.

Per stuffed croissant: 843 cal., 46 g total fat (28 g sat. fat), 253 mg chol., 641 mg sodium, 94 g carbo., 2 g fiber, 13 g pro.

Banana Split Filling with Praline Syrup: Prepare as at left, except substitute 1 tub (8 ounces) cream cheese spread with strawberries for plain cream cheese and 1 medium-size firm, ripe banana, chopped, for the chopped fresh strawberries. Add ½ cup semisweet chocolate pieces with the banana. Omit halved fresh strawberries and maple syrup. Serve with Praline Syrup (below).

Praline Syrup: In small saucepan, combine ¼ cup dark corn syrup and ¼ cup maple-flavored syrup; heat through. Stir in ½ cup toasted chopped pecans.

Peach Filling with Berry Syrup: Prepare as at left, except substitute 1 tub (8 ounces) cream cheese spread with pineapple for plain cream cheese. Substitute 1 medium-size peach or nectarine, pitted and chopped, for the chopped strawberries. Omit halved strawberries and maple syrup. Use Berry Syrup (below).

Berry Syrup: Combine ½ cup maple syrup, maple-flavored syrup or berry syrup and 1 cup blueberries, raspberries and/or sliced strawberries. If desired, warm in saucepan or microwave.

Bacon Filling with Maple Syrup: Prepare as at left, except substitute 1 tub (8 ounces) cream cheese spread with garden vegetables for plain cream cheese, reduce maple syrup to 1 tablespoon and omit chopped and halved strawberries. Add 4 strips crisp-cooked bacon, crumbled, to cream cheese. Drizzle with maple syrup.

Other Variations: Substitute one of the following for the strawberries in Step 1:
- Soak ½ cup raisins in ¼ cup orange juice for 30 minutes; drain and add to cream cheese with ½ teaspoon finely shredded orange peel
- ½ cup chopped tart apple and ¼ cup shredded sharp Cheddar cheese
- ¼ cup chopped, pitted dried dates or dried pineapple and ¼ cup shredded coconut

Banana-Pecan Waffles

As you finish baking each waffle, keep them warm in a 300° oven. Just be sure to put them in a single layer on a large baking sheet or tray, rather than stacking them on a plate. Stacking creates steam, which can make the waffles soggy.

PREP: 20 minutes
COOK: 3 to 4 minutes per waffle
MAKES: about 9 waffles

1¾ cups all-purpose flour
  2 tablespoons granulated sugar
  1 tablespoon baking powder
  ½ teaspoon ground cinnamon
  ¼ teaspoon salt
  2 small bananas, mashed (¾ cup)
  2 eggs, lightly beaten
  1 cup milk
  ¼ cup vegetable oil or melted butter
  1 teaspoon vanilla extract
  ½ cup finely chopped pecans, toasted
     Butter, maple syrup, caramel ice-cream topping,
     sliced bananas and/or chopped, toasted pecans,
     for serving (optional)

1. In large bowl, stir together flour, granulated sugar, baking powder, cinnamon and salt. Make a well in center of flour mixture. Set aside.

2. In medium-size bowl, beat together banana and eggs. Stir in milk, oil and vanilla. Add banana mixture all at once to the flour mixture. Stir just until moistened (batter should be slightly lumpy). Stir in ½ cup pecans.

3. Lightly grease waffle baker. Add batter to waffle baker according to manufacturer's directions. Bake according to manufacturer's directions for 3 to 4 minutes or until golden brown. With a fork, lift waffle off grid. Repeat with remaining batter. Serve warm* with desired toppings.

*Note: To keep prepared waffles warm, place in oven at 300°.

Per waffle: 241 cal., 12 g total fat (2 g sat. fat), 49 mg chol., 172 mg sodium, 28 g carbo., 2 g fiber, 5 g pro.

Blueberry Streusel Coffee Cake

Sour cream in the batter makes this cinnamon-scented and blueberry-studded cake super moist and rich tasting. Universally popular, it is absolutely delicious with a cup of fresh-brewed coffee.

PREP: 30 minutes
BAKE: at 350° for 35 to 40 minutes
MAKES: 16 servings

Cake:
1½ cups packed brown sugar
1 cup coarsely chopped nuts
4 teaspoons ground cinnamon
1 carton (8 ounces) sour cream
1 teaspoon baking soda
½ cup (1 stick) butter, softened
¾ cup granulated sugar
3 eggs
1 teaspoon vanilla extract
2 cups all-purpose flour
1½ teaspoons baking powder
2 cups fresh or frozen blueberries, thawed

Confectioners' Sugar Icing:
½ cup confectioners' sugar
2 teaspoons milk
¼ teaspoon vanilla extract

1. Cake: Heat oven to 350°. Grease bottom and ½ inch up sides of 13×9×2-inch baking pan; set aside. In small bowl, combine brown sugar, nuts and cinnamon. Set aside. In another small bowl, stir together sour cream and baking soda; set aside.

2. In large mixing bowl, combine butter and granulated sugar; beat with electric mixer on medium speed until well mixed. Beat in eggs and 1 teaspoon vanilla until well mixed. Add flour and baking powder; beat until well mixed. Add sour cream mixture; beat until well mixed.

3. Spread half of the batter into prepared pan. Sprinkle blueberries over batter. Sprinkle half of the nut mixture over the blueberries. Carefully spread remaining batter over the topping; sprinkle with remaining nut mixture.

4. Bake at 350° for 35 to 40 minutes or until wooden toothpick inserted near center comes out clean. Place cake on wire rack.

5. Confectioners' Sugar Icing: In small bowl, combine confectioners' sugar, milk and ¼ teaspoon vanilla. Stir in enough additional milk, 1 teaspoon at a time, to make icing of drizzling consistency. Drizzle icing over cake. Serve warm or cool on wire rack.

Per serving: 345 cal., 14 g total fat (6 g sat. fat), 61 mg chol., 182 mg sodium, 52 g carbo., 2 g fiber, 5 g pro.

Maple Bran Muffins

With just a small amount of oil (it's the buttermilk that makes them moist), these hearty, high-fiber, maple-flavored muffins are so delicious, you'll scarcely suspect they're good for you. At just 216 calories for a Texas-sized muffin, they're a real deal.

PREP: 25 minutes
BAKE: at 350° for 25 to 30 minutes
COOL: 5 to 10 minutes
MAKES: 6 large muffins or 12 standard-size muffins

2⅔ **cups whole-bran cereal**
1⅔ **cups buttermilk**
 1 **cup whole wheat flour**
1¾ **teaspoons baking powder**
 ¼ **teaspoon baking soda**
 3 **tablespoons vegetable oil**
 2 **tablespoons (¼ stick) butter, softened**
 ⅓ **cup packed brown sugar**
 2 **eggs**
 ¼ **cup pure maple syrup or maple-flavored syrup**
 ¾ **cup raisins or mixed dried fruit bits**

1. Heat oven to 350°. Lightly grease 6 cups of large-size (3¼-inch) muffin pans or 12 cups of standard muffin pans; set aside. Place bran cereal in medium-size bowl. Pour buttermilk over cereal; let stand for 5 to 10 minutes or until cereal is softened. In small bowl, stir together flour, baking powder and baking soda; set aside.

2. In large mixing bowl, beat oil and butter with electric mixer on medium speed for 30 seconds. Add brown sugar; beat about 30 seconds or until fluffy. Beat in eggs, one at a time, until mixed. Add maple syrup; beat until combined.

3. Add cereal mixture and flour mixture to egg mixture, stirring just until combined. Stir in raisins. Spoon batter into prepared muffin cups. Fill cups three-fourths full.

4. Bake at 350° for 25 to 30 minutes or until tops are golden and centers are firm to the touch. Cool in muffin cups on wire rack for 5 minutes. Remove muffins to wire rack; serve warm.

Per large muffin: 216 cal., 7 g total fat (2 g sat. fat), 42 mg chol., 240 mg sodium, 39 g carbo., 6 g fiber, 6 g pro.

Banana Crunch Muffins

These sunny muffins are crowned with a crunchy streusel topping. They're delicious with morning coffee or afternoon tea—or with a glass of milk as an after-school snack.

PREP: 25 minutes
BAKE: at 375° for 16 to 18 minutes
COOL: 5 minutes
MAKES: 12 muffins

Topping:
- ¼ **cup all-purpose flour**
- ¼ **cup granulated sugar**
- 2 **tablespoons (¼ stick) butter**
- ¼ **cup chopped pecans**

Muffins:
- 2 **cups all-purpose flour**
- ½ **cup granulated sugar**
- ⅓ **cup packed brown sugar**
- 1½ **teaspoons baking soda**
- ¼ **teaspoon salt**
- ¼ **teaspoon ground cinnamon**
- ¼ **teaspoon ground nutmeg**
- ½ **cup (1 stick) butter**
- 2 **medium-size bananas, mashed (1 cup)**
- 1 **egg, lightly beaten**
- ⅓ **cup milk**

1. Topping: In small bowl, stir together ¼ cup flour and ¼ cup granulated sugar. With a pastry blender, cut in the 2 tablespoons butter until mixture resembles coarse crumbs. Stir in pecans; set topping aside.

2. Muffins: Heat oven to 375°. Grease 12 cups of standard muffin pan; set aside. In large bowl, stir together 2 cups flour, ½ cup granulated sugar, brown sugar, baking soda, salt, cinnamon and nutmeg. With pastry blender, cut in ½ cup butter until mixture resembles coarse crumbs.

3. In medium-size bowl, whisk together bananas, egg and milk. Add egg mixture all at once to flour mixture. Stir just until moistened.

4. Spoon batter into prepared muffin cups. Fill cups three-quarters full. Sprinkle with topping. Bake at 375° for 16 to 18 minutes or until golden and a wooden toothpick inserted in the centers comes out clean. Cool in muffin cups on a wire rack for 5 minutes. Remove from muffin cups. Serve warm.

Per muffin: 285 cal., 12 g total fat (7 g sat. fat), 44 mg chol., 285 mg sodium, 42 g carbo., 1 g fiber, 2 g pro.

Custard Rolls with Orange Icing

Custard Rolls with Orange Icing

These fabulous rolls offer a little change of pace from cinnamon or pecan rolls. Filled with creamy custard and topped with orange icing, they can be served warm or cool.

PREP: 40 minutes
RISE: 1¼ hours
BAKE: at 375° for 20 minutes
COOL: 10 minutes
MAKES: 12 rolls

Custard Filling:
- 2 egg yolks
- ⅓ cup granulated sugar
- ¼ cup cornstarch
- 1½ cups milk
- ⅛ teaspoon salt
- 1 tablespoon butter
- 1 teaspoon vanilla extract

Dough:
- 4½ to 5 cups all-purpose flour
- 1 package active dry yeast
- 1 cup milk
- ½ cup water
- ⅓ cup butter
- 2 tablespoons honey
- 2 tablespoons granulated sugar
- ¾ teaspoon salt
- 1 egg
- 1 teaspoon vanilla extract
- ¾ cup golden raisins

Orange Icing:
- 1½ cups confectioners' sugar
- 2 tablespoons orange juice
- 1 tablespoon butter
- ½ teaspoon vanilla extract

1. Custard Filling: In small bowl, stir together egg yolks, ⅓ cup granulated sugar, cornstarch, ¼ cup of the milk and ⅛ teaspoon salt. In small saucepan, bring remaining 1¼ cups milk to a simmer. Stir half of the milk into egg yolk mixture. Return yolk mixture to saucepan. Cook, stirring constantly, over medium heat until mixture comes to a gentle boil. Cook and stir for 2 minutes more. Remove from heat. Stir in 1 tablespoon butter and 1 teaspoon vanilla (mixture will be thick). Transfer custard to 2-quart baking dish; cover surface with plastic wrap. Refrigerate while preparing dough.

2. Dough: In large mixing bowl, stir together 2 cups of the flour and the yeast; set aside. In small saucepan, heat and stir 1 cup milk, water, ⅓ cup butter, honey, 2 tablespoons granulated sugar and ¾ teaspoon salt just until warm (120° to 130°) and butter almost melts. Add to flour mixture. Add whole egg and 1 teaspoon vanilla. Beat with electric mixer on low to medium speed for 30 seconds, scraping bowl. Beat on high speed for 3 minutes. With wooden spoon, stir in raisins and as much of the remaining flour as you can (dough will be sticky). Cover bowl and let dough rise in a warm place until double (about 45 minutes).

3. Grease extra-large baking sheet; set aside. Punch dough down. Turn dough onto a well-floured surface. Roll dough into 12×18-inch rectangle. Stir Custard Filling. Spread filling over the dough, leaving 1 inch along one of the long sides. Roll up the rectangle, starting from the filled long side. Pinch dough to seal seams. Slice into 12 pieces. Place 2 inches apart, cut sides down, on prepared baking sheet. Cover and let rise in a warm place until nearly double (about 30 minutes).

4. Heat oven to 375°. Bake rolls at 375° about 20 minutes or until golden brown. Transfer to a wire rack. Cool for 10 minutes.

5. Orange Icing: In small, heavy saucepan, combine confectioners' sugar, orange juice and 1 tablespoon butter. Cook and stir over medium heat until warm and smooth. Stir in ½ teaspoon vanilla. Immediately spoon icing over warm rolls. Serve rolls warm or cool. Store any leftover rolls in the refrigerator.

Per roll: 415 cal., 10 g total fat (6 g sat. fat), 75 mg chol., 251 mg sodium, 74 g carbo., 2 g fiber, 8 g pro.

Creamy Cinnamon Rolls

Pouring heavy cream over the top of these rolls before baking creates a yummy, gooey caramel in the pan as they bake. (Gild the lily with powdered sugar icing while they're still warm.)

PREP: 20 minutes
RISE: 1 to 1½ hours
BAKE: at 350° for 20 minutes
MAKES: 20 rolls

- 1 loaf (16 ounces) frozen sweet bread dough, thawed
- 2 tablespoons (¼ stick) butter, melted
- ⅔ cup packed brown sugar
- ½ cup chopped walnuts
- 1 teaspoon ground cinnamon
- ½ cup heavy cream
- ⅔ cup confectioners' sugar
  Milk

1. Lightly grease two 8×1½-inch round baking pans; set aside. On lightly floured surface, roll dough into 20×8-inch rectangle. Brush with melted butter. In small bowl, combine brown sugar, walnuts and cinnamon; sprinkle evenly over dough. Starting from a long side, roll up dough. Moisten edges with water and seal. Cut into 20 slices. Place rolls, cut sides down, in prepared pans. Cover and let rise in a warm place until nearly double, 1 to 1½ hours.

2. Heat oven to 350°. Slowly pour heavy cream over rolls in pans. Bake at 350° about 20 minutes or until golden. Let stand for 1 minute. Loosen edges; invert onto serving plates. Scrape any caramel mixture left in pans onto rolls.

3. In a small bowl, combine confectioners' sugar and enough milk (3 to 4 teaspoons) to make drizzling consistency. Drizzle over warm rolls.

Per roll: 160 cal., 7 g total fat (3 g sat. fat), 16 mg chol., 131 mg sodium, 23 g carbo., 1 g fiber, 3 g pro.

Easy Cinnamon Spirals

Homemade cinnamon rolls don't get any easier than this. Based on refrigerated breadstick dough and glazed with caramel ice-cream topping, you can have fresh-from-the-oven rolls on the table in a matter of minutes.

PREP: 30 minutes
BAKE: at 375° for 12 to 15 minutes
MAKES: 12 rolls

  Nonstick cooking spray
- 2 tubes (11 ounces each) refrigerated breadsticks (24 total)
- ⅓ cup butter, softened
- ¼ cup sugar
- 2 teaspoons ground cinnamon
- ½ cup caramel ice-cream topping

1. Heat oven to 375°. Lightly coat 12 cups of a standard muffin pan with nonstick cooking spray; set aside. Unroll and separate breadsticks. Press each piece of dough to flatten slightly. Press ends of two strips together to make one long strip. Spread strips with some of the butter. In small bowl, stir together sugar and cinnamon. Sprinkle sugar mixture over each strip. Roll up each strip into a spiral, starting from a short side. Place rolls in prepared muffin cups, spiral sides up.

2. Bake spirals at 375° for 12 to 15 minutes or until golden. Remove from muffin cups and place on serving plate. Drizzle with caramel topping. Serve warm.

Per roll: 246 cal., 8 g total fat (5 g sat. fat), 14 mg chol., 443 mg sodium, 40 g carbo., 1 g fiber, 4 g pro.

Breakfast Pizza

Pizza for breakfast? Cool! Especially when it has all the good stuff on it—eggs, bacon, ham, crunchy green pepper, and two kinds of melty cheese. Starting with a prebaked pizza crust means it's a snap to make.

PREP: 25 minutes
BAKE: at 400° for 18 to 24 minutes
MAKES: 6 to 8 servings

- ¼ pound plain or peppered bacon, diced
- ½ cup chopped green pepper
- ¼ cup sliced scallions (2)
- 1 (12-inch) baked pizza crust (such as Boboli)
- 1 tub (8 ounces) cream cheese
- 2 eggs
- 1 cup cubed cooked ham
- 1 cup shredded Cheddar cheese (4 ounces)

1. Heat oven to 400°. In large skillet, cook bacon over medium-low heat until crisp. Remove bacon from skillet with a slotted spoon and drain on paper towels. Drain skillet, reserving about 1 tablespoon drippings. Add green pepper and scallions to drippings in skillet; cook until tender. Drain and set aside.

2. Place pizza crust on large baking sheet; set aside. In small mixing bowl, beat cream cheese just until smooth with an electric mixer on medium speed. Add eggs, one at a time, beating until combined. Spread cream cheese mixture over pizza crust. Sprinkle with bacon pieces, green pepper and scallions. Top with ham.

3. Bake at 400° for 15 to 20 minutes or until cream cheese layer is set. Sprinkle with Cheddar cheese. Bake for 3 to 4 minutes more or until Cheddar cheese is melted. Cut into wedges to serve.

Per serving: 410 cal., 27 g total fat (13 g sat. fat), 126 mg chol., 635 mg sodium, 29 g carbo., 1 g fiber, 16 g pro.

Shrimp Pizza: Prepare as above, except omit bacon. Substitute sweet red peper for green pepper and cook sweet pepper and scallions in 1 tablespoon olive oil. Substitute 5 ounces cooked medium-size shrimp, peeled, deveined and coarsely chopped (1 cup) or 2 cans (4 ounces each) small shrimp, drained, for ham and shredded Mexican-blend cheese for Cheddar cheese. (If desired, substitute 1 can (6 ounces) crab meat, drained, flaked and cartilage removed for the shrimp.)

Mushroom-Artichoke Pizza: Omit bacon, green pepper and scallions. In large skillet, cook 2 cups fresh mushrooms, sliced, in 1 tablespoon olive oil over medium-high heat until golden. Continue as directed, substituting cooked mushrooms for ham and adding ½ cup marinated artichoke hearts, drained and coarsely chopped and ½ cup slivered, roasted sweet red pepper. Substitute shredded Italian-blend cheese for Cheddar cheese.

Mediterranean Frittata

Mediterranean Frittata

A frittata is a kind of open-faced omelette. It's highly adaptable—it can be topped with any kind of vegetables, cheese and meats you like—and makes a great supper with a crisp green salad and some good Italian bread.

PREP: 15 minutes
COOK: 10 minutes
MAKES: 6 servings

- 3 tablespoons olive oil
- 1 large onion, chopped (1 cup)
- 2 cloves garlic, minced
- 8 eggs, lightly beaten
- ¼ cup half-and-half, light cream or milk
- ½ cup crumbled feta cheese (2 ounces)
- ½ cup chopped bottled roasted sweet red peppers
- ½ cup sliced kalamata or pitted ripe olives (optional)
- ¼ cup slivered fresh basil leaves
- ⅛ teaspoon black pepper
- ½ cup onion-and-garlic croutons, coarsely crushed
- 2 tablespoons finely shredded Parmesan cheese
  Fresh basil leaves (optional)

1. Heat broiler. In large broilerproof skillet, heat 2 tablespoons of the olive oil over medium heat. Add onion and garlic; cook just until onion is tender.

2. In large bowl, beat together eggs and half-and-half. Stir in feta cheese, roasted peppers, olives (if desired), slivered basil and black pepper. Pour egg mixture over onion mixture in skillet. Cook over medium heat. As mixture begins to set, run a spatula around edge of the skillet, lifting egg mixture so uncooked portion flows underneath. Continue cooking and lifting edges until egg mixture is almost set (surface will be moist). Reduce heat as necessary to prevent overcooking.

3. In small bowl, combine croutons, Parmesan cheese and the remaining 1 tablespoon of oil; sprinkle mixture over frittata.

4. Broil 4 to 5 inches from heat for 1 to 2 minutes or until top is set and crumbs are golden. Cut frittata in wedges to serve. If desired, garnish with fresh basil.

Per serving: 246 cal., 19 g total fat (5 g sat. fat), 295 mg chol., 383 mg sodium, 8 g carbo., 1 g fiber, 11 g pro.

Southwestern Potato Breakfast Bake

Instead of the usual bread cubes or croutons, this south-of-the-border-inspired breakfast casserole is based on frozen hash brown potatoes. Potatoes olé, anyone?

PREP: 25 minutes
BAKE: at 375° for 30 to 35 minutes
STAND: 10 minutes
MAKES: 8 servings

- Nonstick cooking spray
- ½ package (30 ounces) frozen shredded hash brown potatoes (5 cups)
- ¼ teaspoon seasoned salt
- 1 large onion, chopped (1 cup)
- 1 tablespoon olive oil
- 2 cans (15 ounces each) diced tomatoes and green chiles
- 1 teaspoon chili powder
- ½ teaspoon seasoned salt
- ¼ teaspoon black pepper
- 8 eggs
- ⅓ cup milk
- 1 cup shredded Mexican cheese blend (4 ounces)

1. Heat oven to 375°. Lightly coat a 13×9×2-inch baking dish with nonstick cooking spray. Arrange potatoes evenly in dish; sprinkle with ¼ teaspoon seasoned salt. Set aside.

2. In large skillet, cook onion in hot olive oil until tender. Add undrained tomatoes, chili powder, ½ teaspoon seasoned salt and black pepper. Bring to a boil; reduce heat. Simmer, uncovered, for 10 minutes, stirring occasionally. Spoon over potatoes in dish.

3. In large bowl, beat together eggs and milk with wire whisk or rotary beater; pour evenly over potato mixture in dish. Sprinkle with cheese.

4. Bake, uncovered, at 375° for 30 to 35 minutes or until set. Let stand for 10 minutes before serving.

Per serving: 221 cal., 11 g total fat (5 g sat. fat), 225 mg chol., 635 mg sodium, 17 g carbo., 3 g fiber, 13 g pro.

Morning Pecan Casserole

With a combination of savory, sage-flavored sausage and sweet raisin bread, this breakfast casserole covers all the flavor bases. It's convenient, too; assemble and refrigerate it 8 to 24 hours before baking.

PREP: 25 minutes
CHILL: 8 to 24 hours
BAKE: at 350° for 45 to 50 minutes
STAND: 15 minutes
MAKES: 10 servings

- 1 package (7 ounces) brown-and-serve sausage patties
- 12 slices raisin bread, cubed (about 8 cups)
- 6 eggs
- 3 cups milk
- 1 teaspoon vanilla extract
- ¼ teaspoon ground nutmeg
- ¼ teaspoon ground cinnamon
- 1 cup coarsely chopped pecans
- ½ cup packed brown sugar
- ¼ cup (½ stick) butter, softened
- 2 tablespoons pure maple syrup or maple-flavored syrup

1. Brown the sausage patties following package directions. Cut patties into bite-size pieces. Lightly grease 13×9×2-inch baking dish. Spread bread cubes over bottom of baking dish. Top with sausage pieces.

2. In large bowl, beat together eggs, milk, vanilla, nutmeg and cinnamon with wire whisk or rotary beater. Pour egg mixture over bread and sausage. With back of large metal spoon, lightly press bread to moisten all of it. Cover and refrigerate for at least 8 hours or up to 24 hours.

3. Heat oven to 350°. In small bowl, combine pecans, brown sugar, butter and syrup. Drop by teaspoonfuls over top of egg mixture.

4. Bake, uncovered, at 350° for 45 to 50 minutes or until a knife inserted near the center comes out clean. Let stand for 15 minutes before serving.

Per serving: 408 cal., 24 g total fat (7 g sat. fat), 162 mg chol., 386 mg sodium, 36 g carbo., 2 g fiber, 14 g pro.

Melon and Berries Salad

Melon and Berries Salad

This is one of those dishes that gets better with a few hours' chilling time in the refrigerator to allow the flavors to blend. Just don't add the mint or berries until right before serving so that they stay fresh and vibrant.

PREP: 20 minutes
CHILL: up to 24 hours
MAKES: 4 to 6 servings

- 2 **cups chilled cantaloupe cubes or balls**
- 2 **cups chilled honeydew melon cubes or balls**
- 1 **tablespoon honey**
- 1 **teaspoon fresh lime juice**
- 1 **tablespoon chopped fresh mint**
- 1 **cup fresh blueberries and/or red raspberries**

1. In medium-size bowl, combine cantaloupe and honeydew melon. Drizzle honey and lime juice over melon; gently toss to mix. Cover and refrigerate up to 24 hours.

2. To serve, add mint and toss gently to mix. Sprinkle with fresh berries.

Per serving: 96 cal., 0 g total fat (0 g sat. fat), 0 mg chol., 29 mg sodium, 24 g carbo., 2 g fiber, 1 g pro.

Chapter 3

Meals In Minutes

Enjoy a delicious, home-cooked dinner—even on the busiest nights of the week—with these fast-flavor, no-fuss recipes that go from stove to table in just 30 minutes or less.

Bean and Potato Chowder

Chicken Penne in Smoky
Chili Cream Sauce

Chicken Penne in Smoky Chili Cream Sauce

Chicken recipes have been a boon to Austin, Texas, cook Anna Ginsberg. In 2006, she won the million-dollar prize in the Pillsbury Bake-Off with a chicken recipe—and in 2008, this dish garnered the Grand Prize in the Family Circle 75th Anniversary reader recipe contest. "You just pretty much put everything together," Anna says, "but it tastes so good."

PREP: 10 minutes
COOK: 10 minutes
MAKES: 6 servings

¾ pound penne pasta
1½ tablespoons vegetable oil
1 pound boneless, skinless chicken breasts, cut into ¾-inch chunks
⅓ cup chopped onion
1 teaspoon minced garlic
2 cups purchased Alfredo sauce
1 tablespoon chipotle chiles in adobo sauce
2 teaspoons chili powder
2 teaspoons maple syrup
½ teaspoon salt
8 strips fully cooked bacon, heated in microwave and chopped
2 tablespoons chopped fresh cilantro

1. Cook pasta following package directions. Drain well.

2. While pasta is cooking, heat oil in a large skillet over medium-high heat. Cook chicken in hot oil about 4 minutes or until no longer pink. Remove to a plate and reserve.

3. Reduce heat to medium. Add onion to the skillet and cook for 3 minutes, stirring occasionally. Add garlic and cook for 30 seconds. Stir in Alfredo sauce, chipotle, chili powder, maple syrup and salt. Cook over medium-high heat until bubbly. Stir in the chicken.

4. Return pasta to the pot; stir in the Alfredo and chicken mixture. Spoon pasta mixture onto a large serving platter. Sprinkle with bacon and cilantro.

Note: To reduce calories, fat and sodium, opt for a light Alfredo sauce. For a spicier dish, increase the amount of the chipotle chiles.

Per serving: 674 cal., 38 g total fat (15 g sat. fat), 111 mg chol., 1,130 mg sodium, 44 g carbo., 5 g fiber, 35 g pro.

Warm Chicken and Black Bean Salad with Mango Mojo Dressing

For the 2007 National Chicken Cooking Contest sponsored by the National Chicken Council, Sally Sibthorpe of Shelby Township, Michigan, turned a rotisserie chicken into a warm, vegetable-packed main-dish salad inspired by her travels to Jamaica. The great flavors and ease of preparation earned her a second place finish and a $10,000 prize.

PREP: 25 minutes
COOK: 20 minutes
MAKES: 4 servings

- 2 **tablespoons (¼ stick) butter**
- ½ **cup slivered almonds**
- 1 **cup jasmine rice**
- 2 **cups chicken broth**
- 2 **cups bite-size pieces rotisserie chicken**
- ½ **cup sliced scallions (4)**
- ½ **cup canned black beans, rinsed and drained**
- ½ **cup chopped, peeled avocado**
- ½ **cup chopped sweet red pepper**
- ¼ **cup chopped fresh cilantro leaves**

Mango Mojo Dressing:
- 1 **teaspoon cumin seeds**
- 3 **cloves garlic**
- 1 **small hot red chile, halved and seeded***
- ½ **teaspoon salt**
- ½ **cup cubed, peeled mango**
- ¼ **cup olive oil**
- ¼ **cup orange juice**
- 2 **tablespoons lime juice**

1. In large saucepan, melt butter over medium heat. Add almonds; cook until golden. Add rice; cook for 1 minute. Stir in broth. Bring to a boil; reduce heat. Cover and simmer about 20 minutes or until rice is cooked.

2. To serve, stir chicken, scallions, black beans, avocado, chopped sweet pepper and cilantro into rice mixture. Drizzle with half of the Mango Mojo Dressing; toss to combine. Spoon salad onto a serving dish. Pass remaining dressing.

Mango Mojo Dressing: In heavy, small skillet, toast cumin seeds over medium heat about 2 minutes or until fragrant. In mini food processor, combine toasted cumin seeds, garlic cloves, red chile and salt. Cover and process until combined. Add mango, olive oil, orange juice and lime juice. Cover and process until smooth. Return mixture to skillet and heat until warm.

*Note: Hot chiles contain oils that can burn your skin and eyes. Avoid direct contact with them as much as possible. When working with hot chiles, wear plastic or rubber gloves. If your bare hands do touch chiles, wash your hands well with soap and water.

Per serving: 664 cal., 40 g total fat (10 g sat. fat), 78 mg chol., 1,077 mg sodium, 58 g carbo., 7 g fiber, 24 g pro.

Warm Chicken and Black Bean
Salad with Mango Mojo Dressing

Easy Italian Pepper Steak

Using already frozen, prechopped veggies, prepared tomato sauce, and fresh pasta that cooks in a flash makes this traditionally slow-food dish an option for any day of the week.

START TO FINISH: 25 minutes
MAKES: 4 servings

- 1 package (9 ounces) refrigerated fettuccine
- 1 package (1 pound) frozen pepper stir-fry vegetables (yellow, green and red sweet peppers and onion), thawed and well drained
- 2 tablespoons olive oil
- 2 tablespoons balsamic vinegar
- ¾ pound boneless beef top sirloin steak, cut into thin bite-size strips
- ¼ teaspoon red pepper flakes
- 1 can (15 ounces) tomato sauce with Italian herbs
- 2 tablespoons pine nuts, toasted (optional), for garnish
  Red pepper flakes (optional), for serving

1. In large saucepan, cook fettuccine following package directions; drain well. Return fettuccine to saucepan.

2. While fettuccine is cooking, in large skillet, cook frozen stir-fry vegetables in 1 tablespoon of the hot olive oil over medium-high heat for 2 to 3 minutes or until crisp-tender, stirring occasionally. Carefully add balsamic vinegar; toss to coat. Remove vegetable mixture from skillet. Cover to keep warm.

3. In same skillet, cook beef and ¼ teaspoon red pepper flakes in the remaining 1 tablespoon hot olive oil for 2 to 3 minutes or to desired doneness. Add tomato sauce; heat through.

4. Return vegetable mixture to skillet and heat through. Serve over hot fettuccine. If desired, garnish with pine nuts and pass additional red pepper flakes.

Per serving: 457 cal., 14 g total fat (3 g sat. fat), 55 mg chol., 761 mg sodium, 54 g carbo., 5 g fiber, 29 g pro.

Mexican Beef and Veggies

Take advantage of packaged, precooked rice that can be heated in the microwave, and this healthful, veggie-packed skillet dinner creates just one pan to wash.

PREP: 10 minutes
COOK: 20 minutes
MAKES: 4 to 6 servings

- ¾ pound lean ground beef
- 1 medium (1¼ pounds) butternut squash, peeled, seeded and cubed (about 3 cups)
- 2 cloves garlic, minced
- 1 teaspoon ground cumin
- ½ teaspoon salt
- ⅛ teaspoon ground cinnamon
- 1 can (14½ ounces) diced tomatoes
- 1 medium zucchini, halved lengthwise and sliced ¼ inch thick
- ¼ cup water
- ¼ cup chopped fresh cilantro leaves
- 2 to 3 cups hot cooked white or brown rice
  Hot-pepper sauce (optional)

1. In large skillet, cook ground beef, squash, garlic, cumin, salt and cinnamon over medium heat until beef is brown. Drain off fat.

2. Stir in undrained tomatoes. Bring to a boil; reduce heat. Cover and simmer about 8 minutes or just until squash is tender. Stir in zucchini and water. Cover and simmer about 4 minutes more or until zucchini is tender. Stir in cilantro. Serve over hot cooked rice. If desired, season to taste with hot-pepper sauce.

Per serving: 313 cal., 9 g total fat (3 g sat. fat), 54 mg chol., 504 mg sodium, 39 g carbo., 3 g fiber, 20 g pro.

Simple Beef and Noodles

Canned mushroom soup provides the sauce base for this quick and creamy comfort-food classic.

PREP: 10 minutes
COOK: about 20 minutes
MAKES: 6 servings

- ¾ **pound wide egg noodles (6 cups)**
- 1 **package (17 ounces) refrigerated cooked beef tips with gravy**
- ½ **teaspoon dried basil**
- ¼ **teaspoon black pepper**
- 1 **can (10¾ ounces) condensed golden mushroom soup**
- ½ **cup beef broth**
- 1½ **cups sliced fresh mushrooms**
- 1 **cup packaged peeled baby carrots, halved lengthwise**
- 1 **cup frozen small whole onions**

1. In large saucepan, cook noodles following package directions; drain well. Return noodles to saucepan; cover and keep warm.

2. While noodles are cooking, in another large saucepan, combine beef tips with gravy, basil and pepper. Stir in soup and broth. Bring to a boil. Add mushrooms, carrots and onions. Return to a boil; reduce heat to low. Cover and simmer about 20 minutes or until vegetables are tender, stirring often. Serve meat mixture over noodles.

Per serving: 364 cal., 8 g total fat (2 g sat. fat), 87 mg chol., 903 mg sodium, 51 g carbo., 4 g fiber, 22 g pro.

Asian Beef and Noodle Bowl

Asian Beef and Noodle Bowl

This satisfying one-dish dinner is delicious garnished with a sprinkling of chopped roasted and lightly salted peanuts or cashews.

START TO FINISH: 30 minutes
MAKES: 4 servings

- 4 cups water
- 2 packages (3 ounces each) ramen noodles (any flavor)
- 2 teaspoons chili oil or 2 teaspoons vegetable oil plus ⅛ teaspoon cayenne pepper
- ¾ pound beef flank steak or top round steak, cut into thin bite-size strips
- 1 teaspoon grated fresh ginger
- 2 cloves garlic, minced
- 1 cup beef broth
- 2 tablespoons soy sauce
- 2 cups torn fresh spinach
- 1 cup shredded carrots (2)
- ¼ cup chopped fresh cilantro leaves

1. In large saucepan, bring water to a boil. If desired, break up noodles; drop noodles into the boiling water. (Reserve the flavor packets for another use.) Return to a boil; boil for 2 to 3 minutes or just until noodles are tender but firm, stirring occasionally. Drain noodles; set aside.

2. While the noodles are cooking, in extra-large skillet, heat oil over medium-high heat. Add beef, ginger and garlic; cook and stir for 2 to 3 minutes or until beef is desired doneness. Carefully stir beef broth and soy sauce into skillet. Bring to a boil; reduce heat.

3. Add spinach, carrots, cilantro and cooked noodles to skillet; stir to combine. Heat through.

Per serving: 379 cal., 17 g total fat (3 g sat. fat), 34 mg chol., 1,538 mg sodium, 30 g carbo., 2 g fiber, 26 g pro.

Meatball and Red Pepper Pasta

You don't really even need a vegetable side with this dish—a healthy dose of carrots are cooked right into the sauce. Their sweetness is a nice complement to the mild spiciness of the red pepper sauce.

PREP: 10 minutes
COOK: 20 minutes
MAKES: 6 servings

- ½ **pound spaghetti or bow-tie pasta**
- 2 **medium-size carrots, thinly sliced (1 cup)**
- 1 **medium-size onion, chopped (½ cup)**
- 2 **cloves garlic, minced**
- 1 **tablespoon olive oil or vegetable oil**
- 2 **packages (12 ounces each) frozen cooked Italian-style meatballs (24 meatballs)**
- 1 **jar (26 ounces) spicy red pepper pasta sauce**
  Finely shredded Parmesan cheese

1. In large saucepan, cook pasta following package directions; drain well.

2. While pasta is cooking, in large skillet, cook carrots, onion and garlic in hot oil over medium heat about 5 minutes or just until tender. Stir in meatballs and pasta sauce. Bring to a boil; reduce heat. Cover and simmer about 15 minutes or until meatballs are heated through.

3. Serve meatballs and sauce over hot cooked pasta. Sprinkle with Parmesan cheese.

Per serving including meatballs: 591 cal., 31 g total fat (13 g sat. fat), 77 mg chol., 1,225 mg sodium, 46 g carbo., 8 g fiber, 28 g pro.

Meatballs Stroganoff

A dollop of Dijon adds tangy flavor and a little bit of zing to an otherwise classic stroganoff sauce.

START TO FINISH: 30 minutes
MAKES: 6 to 8 servings

- 1 package (12 to 16 ounces) frozen cooked meatballs
- 1 cup reduced-sodium beef broth
- 1 can (4 ounces drained weight) sliced mushrooms, drained
- 1 carton (8 ounces) sour cream
- 2 tablespoons all-purpose flour
- ½ cup milk
- 1 tablespoon Dijon mustard
- 4 cups hot cooked wide egg noodles
  Chopped fresh parsley leaves (optional)

1. In large skillet, combine meatballs, broth and mushrooms. Bring to a boil; reduce heat. Cover and simmer 15 minutes or until meatballs are heated through.

2. In small bowl, stir together sour cream and flour. Whisk in milk and mustard. Stir sour cream mixture into skillet. Cook and stir until thickened and bubbly. Cook and stir for 1 minute more. Serve over hot cooked noodles. If desired, stir in parsley.

Per serving: 424 cal., 25 g total fat (12 g sat. fat), 73 mg chol., 696 mg sodium, 36 g carbo., 3 g fiber, 16 g pro.

Steak and Mushrooms

As simple as this recipe is (it calls for only five ingredients, not counting salt and pepper), it is elegant enough for company. Serve it, steakhouse style, with sides of fresh spinach sautéed in garlic and herb-roasted potatoes. (They can be frozen—no one will be the wiser.)

PREP: 15 minutes
COOK: 13 to 16 minutes
MAKES: 4 servings

  4 beef tenderloin steaks, cut ¾ inch thick (about
       1 pound total)
       Salt and black pepper
  1 tablespoon olive oil
  3 cups sliced fresh mushrooms (about 8 ounces)
  ¼ cup seasoned beef broth
  ¼ cup heavy cream

1. Sprinkle steaks with salt and pepper. In large skillet, cook steaks in hot oil over medium-high heat for 7 to 9 minutes or to desired doneness (145° for medium rare or 160° for medium), turning once halfway through cooking. Transfer steaks to a serving platter and keep warm.

2. In the same skillet, cook and stir mushrooms over medium-high heat for 4 to 5 minutes or until tender. Stir in broth and heavy cream. Cook and stir over medium-high heat for 2 minutes. Season sauce to taste with additional salt and pepper. Spoon mushroom mixture over steaks to serve.

Per steak + about ¼ cup sauce: 279 cal., 19 g total fat (7 g sat. fat), 90 mg chol., 189 mg sodium, 3 g carbo., 1 g fiber, 26 g pro.

Chicken with Skillet Gravy

Chicken and gravy may sound like a Sunday supper that takes all day to cook, but this quick version—made with boneless, skinless chicken breasts and in a skillet on the stovetop—takes just minutes.

PREP: 20 minutes
COOK: 12 to 15 minutes
MAKES: 4 servings

  ⅓ cup fine dry seasoned bread crumbs
  2 tablespoons grated Parmesan cheese
  ½ teaspoon paprika
  1 egg, lightly beaten
  2 tablespoons milk
  4 boneless, skinless chicken breast halves (about
       1¼ pounds total)
       Salt and black pepper (optional)
  2 tablespoons vegetable oil
  3 tablespoons butter
  3 tablespoons all-purpose flour
  ¼ teaspoon dried sage
  1 can (14 ounces) chicken broth
  1 package (16 ounces) refrigerated mashed
       potatoes, heated following package directions

1. In shallow dish, combine bread crumbs, Parmesan cheese and paprika; set aside. In another shallow dish, combine egg and milk. If desired, sprinkle chicken lightly with salt and pepper. Dip chicken into egg mixture, then coat with crumb mixture.

2. In heavy, large skillet, heat oil over medium-high heat until a few bread crumbs sizzle when added to pan.

3. Add chicken to skillet. Cook, uncovered, over medium heat for 12 to 15 minutes or until no longer pink (170°), turning once. Transfer to serving platter; keep warm.

4. For gravy, melt butter in skillet. Stir in flour and sage. Add chicken broth. Cook and stir over medium heat until thickened and bubbly; cook and stir for 1 minute more. Season to taste with additional salt and pepper. Serve with chicken and mashed potatoes.

Per serving: 528 cal., 27 g total fat (12 g sat. fat), 180 mg chol., 988 mg sodium, 28 g carbo., 2 g fiber, 42 g pro.

Chicken Linguine with Pesto Sauce

Purchased pesto comes in off-the-shelf glass jars and in refrigerated containers. If you can find the refrigerated kind, opt for that. It generally tastes fresher and has better color and flavor.

START TO FINISH: 20 minutes
MAKES: 4 servings

- ½ pound linguine
- 1 package (10 ounces) frozen broccoli, cauliflower and carrots
- 1 container (10 ounces) refrigerated Alfredo pasta sauce or 1 cup bottled Alfredo sauce
- ⅓ cup purchased basil pesto
- ¼ cup milk
- ½ of a rotisserie chicken (2 to 2¼ pounds)
  Milk (optional)
  Grated Parmesan cheese

1. In 4- to 5-quart Dutch oven, cook pasta following package directions, adding vegetables during the last 5 minutes of cooking. Drain well. Return pasta mixture to Dutch oven.

2. While pasta and vegetables are cooking, in small bowl, combine Alfredo sauce, pesto and ¼ cup milk; set aside. Remove meat from chicken (discard skin and bones); chop or shred meat.

3. Add chicken to pasta and vegetables in Dutch oven. Add sauce mixture; toss gently to coat. Heat through over medium-low heat. If desired, stir in additional milk to reach desired consistency. Sprinkle each serving with Parmesan cheese.

Per serving: 801 cal., 48 g total fat (4 g sat. fat), 109 mg chol., 546 mg sodium, 54 g carbo., 3 g fiber, 37 g pro.

Chicken and Spinach Pasta Toss

Santa Fe Chicken and Vegetables

Cooked chicken breast is a handy thing to have in your refrigerator for tossing in salads, slicing for sandwiches or pizza toppings—or turning into a super-quick pasta dinner. Next time you're grilling or roasting chicken breasts, toss in a couple of extra. Cool completely, then wrap tightly and store in the refrigerator for 3 to 4 days.

START TO FINISH: 20 minutes
MAKES: 4 servings

- ½ pound whole wheat linguine
  Nonstick cooking spray
- 2 cloves garlic, minced
- 4 cups torn fresh spinach
- 2 cups chopped cooked chicken
- 1 cup reduced-sodium chicken broth
- ¼ cup snipped dried tomatoes (not oil packed)
- 1 tablespoon lemon juice
- 1 tablespoon finely shredded lemon peel
- 2 tablespoons pine nuts, toasted
- ¼ teaspoon black pepper
- ¼ cup freshly grated Parmesan cheese

1. Cook pasta following package directions; drain well. Return pasta to saucepan; cover and keep warm.

2. Whle the pasta is cooking, lightly coat large skillet with nonstick cooking spray. Heat skillet over medium heat. Add garlic to skillet; cook and stir for 30 seconds. Add spinach, chicken, broth, tomatoes and lemon juice to skillet. Cook, stirring frequently, for 4 to 5 minutes or until spinach wilts. Add chicken mixture to pasta. Add lemon peel, pine nuts and pepper; toss gently to combine. Transfer to a serving dish; sprinkle with Parmesan cheese.

Per serving: 405 cal., 11 g total fat (3 g sat. fat), 67 mg chol., 379 mg sodium, 48 g carbo., 1 g fiber, 33 g pro.

If you can find them, try using a can of fire-roasted diced tomatoes in place of the can of regular ones. They're a little more expensive, but they do add a lot of extra flavor.

PREP: 10 minutes
COOK: about 15 minutes
MAKES: 6 servings

- 1 can (14 ounces) chicken broth
- ¼ cup water
- 2 cups couscous
- 1 sweet red pepper, seeded and chopped
- ⅓ cup chopped onion (1 small)
- 2 teaspoons olive oil
- 1 cup frozen broccoli florets
- 1 cup frozen whole kernel corn
- 2 cups cubed cooked chicken
- 1 can (15 ounces) black beans, rinsed and drained
- 1 can (14½ ounces) diced tomatoes
- 1 teaspoon ground cumin
- 1 cup shredded Monterey Jack cheese (4 ounces)
- 1 tablespoon chopped fresh cilantro leaves

1. In medium saucepan, bring broth and water to a boil. Stir in couscous and remove from heat. Cover and let stand for 5 minutes.

2. While couscous is standing, in large skillet, cook sweet pepper and onion in hot oil over medium heat for 5 minutes, stirring occasionally. Stir in broccoli and corn. Cook for 3 minutes more, stirring occasionally.

3. Add chicken, beans, undrained tomatoes and cumin to skillet. Cook for 3 to 5 minutes or until heated through. Serve chicken mixture over couscous. Sprinkle with cheese and cilantro.

Per serving: 737 cal., 12 g total fat (5 g sat. fat), 59 mg chol., 738 mg sodium, 117 g carbo., 12 g fiber, 41 g pro.

Greek-Style Lamb Skillet

Spicing meat with cinnamon—as is done here—is not uncommon in Greek and Middle Eastern cooking. It adds a subtle warmth and just a little sweetness to the dish.

PREP: 10 minutes
COOK: 20 minutes
MAKES: 4 servings

- ¾ pound ground lamb or ground beef
- 1 can (14½ ounces) diced tomatoes with onion and garlic
- 1 can (5½ ounces) tomato juice
- ½ cup onion-flavored beef broth
- ½ teaspoon ground cinnamon
- 1 cup medium-size shell macaroni or elbow macaroni
- 1 cup frozen cut green beans
- ½ cup crumbled feta cheese (about 2 ounces)

1. In large skillet, cook ground meat over medium heat until brown. Drain off fat. Add undrained tomatoes, tomato juice, broth and cinnamon; mix well. Bring to a boil.

2. Stir in uncooked macaroni and green beans. Return to a boil; reduce heat. Cover and simmer for 15 to 20 minutes or until macaroni and green beans are tender. Sprinkle with feta cheese.

Per serving: 451 cal., 24 g total fat (12 g sat. fat), 79 mg chol., 927 mg sodium, 35 g carbo., 3 g fiber, 22 g pro.

Potato Cake with Sausage and Apples

This is the perfect dish for a cool fall night. Enjoy it with a glass of beer or apple cider.

PREP: 10 minutes
COOK: about 20 minutes
MAKES: 4 servings

- 2 tablespoons olive oil
- 2 tablespoons (¼ stick) butter
- ½ of a package (26 ounces) frozen shredded hash brown potatoes (about 5 cups)
- 1 tablespoon chopped fresh thyme leaves or 1 teaspoon dried thyme
- ¼ teaspoon black pepper
- 6 ounces cooked smoked sausage, coarsely chopped
- 1 medium-size apple, such as Golden Delicious, cut into thin wedges
  Salt

1. In 10-inch cast-iron or nonstick skillet, heat olive oil and 1 tablespoon of the butter over medium heat. Add potatoes in an even layer. Cook about 8 minutes or until lightly browned, stirring occasionally. Stir in half the thyme and the pepper. Firmly press down potato mixture with a wide metal spatula. Cook about 8 minutes more or until potatoes are tender.

2. While potato mixture cooks, in medium skillet, melt remaining 1 tablespoon butter over medium heat. Add sausage and apple. Cook about 10 minutes or until apple is tender, stirring occasionally. Stir in remaining thyme.

3. Unmold potatoes onto serving platter; top with sausage mixture. Season to taste with salt.

Per serving: 366 cal., 28 g total fat (10 g sat. fat), 47 mg chol., 527 mg sodium, 21 g carbo., 2 g fiber, 8 g pro.

Oriental Pork and Vegetables

If you use rice stick noodles, you'll have to soak them in hot water before using them. Just follow the directions on the package.

PREP: 10 minutes
COOK: about 8 minutes
MAKES: 4 servings

  1 **pork tenderloin (¾ pound)**
  6 **ounces rice stick noodles or 2 packages (3 ounces each) ramen noodles (any flavor), broken, if desired**
  2 **teaspoons dark Asian sesame oil or olive oil**
  1 **package (1 pound) frozen stir-fry vegetables**
  ¼ **cup teriyaki sauce**
  2 **tablespoons plum sauce**

1. Cut meat into ¼-inch strips; set aside.

2. Discard spice packet from ramen noodles, if using, or save for another use. Prepare noodles following package directions. Set aside and keep warm.

3. Heat 12-inch nonstick skillet over medium-high heat. Add 1 teaspoon of the sesame oil. Add vegetables to skillet; cook and stir for 4 to 6 minutes or until crisp-tender. Remove vegetables from skillet. Set aside and keep warm.

4. Add remaining oil to skillet. Add pork; cook over medium-high heat for 4 to 6 minutes or until no longer pink, turning to brown evenly. Stir in vegetables (drained, if necessary), teriyaki sauce and plum sauce; heat through. Toss meat mixture with noodles.

Per serving: 341 cal., 5 g total fat (1 g sat. fat), 55 mg chol., 820 mg sodium, 48 g carbo., 3 g fiber, 22 g pro.

Oriental Beef and Vegetables: Prepare as above, except substitute 1 boneless beef top round or sirloin steak (¾ pound) for pork tenderloin.

Per serving beef variation: 350 cal., 6 g total fat (1 g sat. fat), 48 mg chol., 830 mg sodium, 48 g carbo.,3 g fiber, 23 g pro.

Italian-Style Fish

Use any white-fleshed fish for this dish. Good choices include cod, halibut, sea bass, tilapia or orange roughy.

PREP: 15 minutes
BROIL: 4 to 6 minutes per ½-inch thickness fish
MAKES: 6 servings

1½   pounds fresh or frozen white-fleshed fish fillets,
    ½ to 1 inch thick
¼   teaspoon salt
⅛   teaspoon black pepper
2   cups sliced fresh mushrooms
1   tablespoon vegetable oil
1   can (14½ ounces) Italian-style stewed tomatoes
1   can (10¾ ounces) condensed tomato bisque soup
⅛   teaspoon black pepper
⅓   cup finely shredded Parmesan cheese
    Hot cooked pasta

1. Thaw fish, if frozen. Preheat broiler. Rinse fish; pat dry with paper towels. If necessary, cut fish into 6 serving-size pieces. Measure thickness of fish. Place fish on the greased, unheated rack of a broiler pan. Turn any thin portions under to make uniform thickness. Sprinkle with salt and ⅛ teaspoon pepper.

2. Broil about 4 inches from the heat until fish flakes easily when tested with a fork. Allow 4 to 6 minutes per ½-inch thickness of fish. (If fillets are 1 inch thick, turn once halfway through broiling.)

3. While fish is cooking, in medium-size saucepan, cook mushrooms in hot oil until tender. Stir in stewed tomatoes, soup and ⅛ teaspoon pepper. Cook and stir over medium heat until mixture is heated through.

4. Spoon hot tomato mixture over fish fillets. Sprinkle with Parmesan cheese. Serve with hot cooked pasta.

Per serving: 415 cal., 14 g total fat (6 g sat. fat), 71 mg chol., 1,218 mg sodium, 35 g carbo., 2 g fiber, 37 g pro.

Pan-Fried Tilapia Fillets

With the exception of the fish, these flash-in-the-pan fillets are made with ingredients you likely have on hand in your pantry and refrigerator—so it's not just the cooking that goes fast, but the shopping, too.

PREP: 20 minutes
COOK: 6 to 8 minutes
MAKES: 4 servings

4   fresh or frozen tilapia fillets, about ½ inch thick
    (6 to 8 ounces each)
1   cup toasted wheat germ
½   cup grated Parmesan cheese
1   teaspoon dried Italian seasoning
1   teaspoon paprika
¾   teaspoon salt
½   teaspoon garlic powder
½   teaspoon dried basil
¼   teaspoon black pepper
2   egg whites, lightly beaten
¼   cup skim milk
2   tablespoons canola oil

1. Thaw fish, if frozen. Rinse fish; pat dry with paper towels. In shallow dish, combine wheat germ, Parmesan cheese, Italian seasoning, paprika, salt, garlic powder, basil and pepper. In another shallow dish, stir together egg whites and milk. Dip fillets in egg white mixture. Coat both sides with wheat germ mixture.

2. In 12-inch skillet, cook fish in hot canola oil over medium heat for 6 to 8 minutes or until coating is golden and fish flakes easily when tested with a fork, turning once. (Reduce heat as necessary to prevent burning.)

Per serving: 387 cal., 15 g total fat (4 g sat. fat), 94 mg chol., 715 mg sodium, 17 g carbo., 4 g fiber, 47 g pro.

Shrimp and Ramen Noodle Stir-Fry

Bags of frozen peeled and deveined frozen shrimp are a good thing to have in the freezer. They defrost easily. Just put them—still sealed in the bag—in a sinkful of cool water for 20 to 30 minutes or until they're completely defrosted.

PREP: 20 minutes
COOK: 5 minutes
MAKES: 4 servings

- ¾ pound fresh or frozen peeled and deveined cooked shrimp or tub-style firm tofu, drained and cubed
- 2 packages (3 ounces each) shrimp- or mushroom-flavored ramen noodles
- 2 teaspoons dark Asian sesame oil or vegetable oil
- 1 tablespoon vegetable oil
- 1 medium-size sweet red or yellow pepper, cut into thin strips
- ¾ cup fresh pea pods, strings and tips removed, or ½ of a package (6 ounces) frozen pea pods, thawed
- 2 cups chopped bok choy
- ½ cup chopped scallions (4)
- ¼ cup hoisin sauce or bottled stir-fry sauce
- ¼ cup orange juice
- ¼ teaspoon red pepper flakes (optional)
- 2 teaspoons sesame seeds, toasted*

1. Thaw shrimp, if frozen. Remove tails. Rinse shrimp; pat dry with paper towels. Set aside. In large saucepan, cook noodles with seasoning following package directions. Drain noodles. Return noodles to pan and toss with sesame oil. Cut noodles with kitchen scissors for shorter lengths. Set aside.

2. In large skillet, heat 1 tablespoon vegetable oil over medium-high heat. Add sweet pepper strips and stir-fry for 2 minutes. Add pea pods and bok choy; stir-fry for 2 minutes. Add shrimp, scallions, hoisin sauce, orange juice and, if desired, red pepper flakes. Stir-fry for 1 minute.

3. To serve, place noodles on serving plates. Spoon the shrimp mixture over noodles and sprinkle with toasted sesame seeds.

*Note: To toast sesame seeds, in ungreased shallow baking pan, spread seeds in thin layer. Bake at 350° for 10 to 15 minutes or until lightly toasted, stirring twice.

Per serving: 406 cal., 17 g total fat (1 g sat. fat), 130 mg chol., 1,233 mg sodium, 41 g carbo., 3 g fiber, 25 g pro.

Curried Shrimp in Peanut Sauce Pasta

Curried Shrimp in Peanut Sauce Pasta

Toasting coconut can be a little tricky—it burns quickly. Spread it in a thin layer on a rimmed baking sheet and place it in a 350° oven for 2 to 4 minutes—stirring every 30 seconds or so—until it's mostly light brown with a few remaining white shreds.

START TO FINISH: 30 minutes
MAKES: 4 servings

- 1 **pound fresh or frozen peeled, deveined large shrimp**
- ¼ **cup reduced-sodium soy sauce**
- 1 **tablespoon curry powder**
- ¼ **teaspoon red pepper flakes**
- 6 **cloves garlic, minced**
- ½ **pound fettuccine or linguine**
- ½ **cup frozen peas**
- ⅓ **cup reduced-sodium chicken broth**
- ¼ **cup unsweetened coconut milk**
- 2 **tablespoons creamy peanut butter**
- 1 **tablespoon olive oil**
- 2 **tablespoons sliced scallions (1), for garnish**
  Toasted coconut, for garnish

1. Thaw shrimp, if frozen. In medium-size bowl, toss shrimp with soy sauce, curry powder, red pepper flakes and garlic; set aside.

2. In large saucepan, cook pasta following package directions, adding the peas for the last minute of cooking. Drain well; set aside.

3. In the same saucepan, combine broth, coconut milk and peanut butter. Heat over medium-low heat until nearly smooth and bubbly, whisking constantly. Add drained pasta mixture; toss to coat. Keep warm.

4. In large skillet, cook shrimp mixture in hot oil over medium-high heat for 2 to 4 minutes or until shrimp turn pink. To serve, divide pasta mixture among serving plates. Top with shrimp mixture. Garnish with sliced scallion and toasted coconut.

Per serving: 492 cal., 15 g total fat (6 g sat. fat), 172 mg chol., 864 mg sodium, 53 g carbo., 4 g fiber, 36 g pro.

Bean and Potato Chowder

Creamy and rich, this soul-satisfying soup—with its accompanying cheese toast—needs only a crisp green salad to be a complete meal.

START TO FINISH: 20 minutes
MAKES: 4 servings

- 1 package (20 ounces) refrigerated diced potatoes with onions
- 1 can (14 ounces) vegetable broth
- ⅓ cup all-purpose flour
- 1 cup shredded Swiss cheese (4 ounces)
- 3 cups milk
- 1 teaspoon dried Italian seasoning
- 1 can (15 ounces) navy beans, rinsed and drained
  Salt and black pepper
  Bottled roasted sweet red pepper and chopped fresh parsley leaves (optional)
- 8 ½-inch slices Italian bread topped with shredded Swiss cheese, toasted (optional)

1. In 4-quart Dutch oven, combine potatoes and vegetable broth; cover and bring to a boil over high heat. Reduce heat. Simmer, covered, for 4 minutes. In large bowl, toss together flour and 1 cup of the shredded cheese until cheese is coated. Gradually stir in milk until combined. Add milk mixture and Italian seasoning to potato mixture. Cook and stir over medium heat until thickened and bubbly. Stir in beans; cook and stir for 1 minute more. Season to taste with salt and pepper. If desired, top with sweet pepper and parsley and serve with cheese-topped bread.

Per serving: 494 cal., 12 g total fat (7 g sat. fat), 41 mg chol., 1,344 mg sodium, 70 g carbo., 9 g fiber, 25 g pro.

Mushrooms and Pasta

Never wash mushrooms under running water—they get waterlogged. Clean them by brushing them off gently with a damp paper towel, then trim the ends off of the stems.

START TO FINISH: 30 minutes
MAKES: 4 servings

- 3 tablespoons butter
- 1 tablespoon olive oil
- 1 medium-size onion, chopped (½ cup)
- 3 cloves garlic, minced
- ¾ pound fresh button mushrooms, halved or quartered (4½ cups)
- 1 tablespoon chopped fresh thyme or 1 teaspoon dried thyme
- ½ teaspoon salt
- ¼ teaspoon black pepper
- ½ cup heavy cream
- ½ cup finely shredded Parmesan cheese (2 ounces)
- 3 cups hot cooked pasta
  Chopped fresh parsley leaves (optional)

1. In large skillet, heat butter and olive oil over medium heat. Add onion and garlic. Cook for 4 to 5 minutes or until onion is tender, stirring occasionally. Stir in mushrooms, thyme, salt and black pepper. Cook for 4 to 5 minutes more or until mushrooms are tender and lightly browned, stirring occasionally. Add heavy cream. Bring just to a boil; reduce heat. Boil gently, uncovered, for 2 to 3 minutes or until thickened. Stir in Parmesan cheese until melted.

2. To serve, place hot cooked pasta in serving bowl. Spoon mushroom sauce over pasta. If desired, sprinkle with parsley.

Per serving: 425 cal., 27 g total fat (15 g sat. fat), 71 mg chol., 539 mg sodium, 36 g carbo., 3 g fiber, 12 g pro.

Ravioli Skillet

Starting with Italian-style stewed tomatoes gives this dish a flavor boost before you even begin cooking. A sprinkle of chopped fresh basil right before serving is a final flourish.

PREP: 5 minutes
COOK: about 15 minutes
MAKES: 4 servings

- 1 can (14½ ounces) Italian-style stewed tomatoes
- ½ cup water
- 2 medium-size zucchini and/or yellow summer squash, halved lengthwise and sliced ½ inch thick
- 1 package (9 ounces) refrigerated whole wheat four-cheese ravioli
- 1 can (15 or 16 ounces) cannellini (white kidney) beans or navy beans, rinsed and drained
- 2 tablespoons chopped fresh basil or parsley leaves
- 2 tablespoons finely shredded or grated Parmesan cheese

1. In very large skillet, combine undrained tomatoes and the water; bring to a boil. Add zucchini and/or yellow summer squash and ravioli. Return to a boil; reduce heat. Cover and boil gently for 6 to 7 minutes or until ravioli is tender, stirring gently once or twice.

2. Stir beans into ravioli mixture; heat through. Sprinkle with basil and Parmesan cheese.

Per serving: 305 cal., 8 g total fat (4 g sat. fat), 44 mg chol., 986 mg sodium, 49 g carbo., 11 g fiber, 18 g pro.

Chapter 4

Cook It Slowly

Too busy to cook? Let your slow cooker do it for you. Fill it with fresh ingredients before you leave home for the day, and come back to the welcome smell of a delicious dinner that's ready to eat.

Hot Kielbasa and Potato Salad

Southwestern Bean Soup with
Cornmeal Dumplings

Southwestern Bean Soup with Cornmeal Dumplings

Fluffy cornmeal dumplings top off this hearty but healthful vegetarian soup.

PREP: 15 minutes
COOK: 10 to 12 hours plus 30 minutes on low-heat setting
MAKES: 6 servings

- 3 cups water
- 1 can (15 ounces) red kidney beans, rinsed and drained
- 1 can (15 ounces) black beans, pinto beans, or Great Northern beans, rinsed and drained
- 1 14½-ounce can Mexican-style stewed tomatoes
- 1 10-ounce package frozen whole kernel corn
- 1 cup sliced carrot
- 1 cup chopped onion
- 1 can (4 ounces) diced green chiles
- 2 tablespoons instant beef or chicken bouillon granules
- 1 to 2 teaspoons chili powder
- 2 cloves garlic, minced
- ⅓ cup all-purpose flour
- ¼ cup yellow cornmeal
- 1 teaspoon baking powder
  Dash salt
  Dash black pepper
- 1 beaten egg white
- 2 tablespoons milk
- 1 tablespoon vegetable oil

1. In 3½- or 4-quart slow cooker combine water, beans, undrained tomatoes, corn, carrot, onion, undrained chiles, bouillon granules, chili powder and garlic. Cover and cook on low-heat setting for 10 to 12 hours.

2. In medium mixing bowl, stir together flour, cornmeal, baking powder, salt and pepper. In a small mixing bowl combine egg white, milk and oil. Add to flour mixture; stir with a fork just until combined. Drop dumpling mixture into 6 mounds atop the bubbling soup. Cover and cook for 30 minutes more. (Do not lift lid while dumplings are cooking.)

Per serving: 270 cal., 3 g total fat (1 g sat. fat), 1 mg chol., 1,593 mg sodium, 54 g carbo., 15 g pro.

Broccoli Cheese Soup

This fix-and-forget version of this favorite soup means you can enjoy it any day of the week—no matter how busy you are.

PREP: 25 minutes
COOK: 5 to 6 hours on low-heat setting or 2½ to 3 hours on high-heat setting
MAKES: 6 main-dish servings

- 6 **cups chopped broccoli stems and florets**
- 2 **small potatoes, peeled and chopped (1½ cups)**
- 1 **medium-size onion, chopped (½ cup)**
- 2 **cloves garlic, minced**
- ⅛ **teaspoon cayenne pepper**
- 3 **cans (14 ounces each) reduced-sodium chicken broth**
- 8 **ounces process American cheese, cut into ½-inch cubes**
- ½ **cup shredded sharp Cheddar cheese (2 ounces)**
- 1 **cup half-and-half or light cream**

1. In 3½- or 4-quart slow cooker, combine broccoli, potatoes, onion, garlic and cayenne pepper. Pour broth over all.

2. Cover slow cooker; cook on low-heat setting for 5 to 6 hours or on high-heat setting for 2½ to 3 hours.

3. Add American cheese and Cheddar cheese, stirring until melted; stir in half-and-half.

Per serving: 310 cal., 20 g total fat (13 g sat. fat), 62 mg chol., 1,150 mg sodium, 16 g carbo., 3 g fiber, 18 g pro.

Beef and Chipotle Burritos

This dish makes great casual party fare. You can clean the house while it cooks—and guests can make up their own burritos with the flavor of tortilla they like, cheese and fresh Pico de Gallo Salsa.

PREP: 35 minutes
COOK: 8 to 10 hours on low-heat setting or 4 to 5 hours on high-heat setting
MAKES: 8 burritos

Pico de Gallo Salsa:
- 1 **cup finely chopped fresh tomatoes (2 medium-size)**
- 2 **tablespoons finely chopped onion**
- 2 **tablespoons chopped fresh cilantro leaves**
- 1 **fresh serrano chile, seeded and finely chopped***
- ½ **cup chopped, peeled jicama**
- ¼ **cup radishes cut into thin bite-size strips**

Filling:
- 1½ **pounds boneless beef round steak, cut ¾ inch thick**
- 2 **cans (14½ ounces each) diced tomatoes with garlic and onion**
- 2 **canned chipotle chiles in adobo sauce, finely chopped***
- 1 **teaspoon dried oregano**
- ¼ **teaspoon ground cumin**

Burritos:
- 8 **(7- to 8-inch) whole wheat, plain or tomato-flavored flour tortillas, warmed**
- ¾ **cup shredded reduced-fat Cheddar cheese (3 ounces)**

1. Pico de Gallo Salsa: In small bowl, combine tomatoes, onion, cilantro and serrano chile. Stir in jicama and radishes. Cover; refrigerate several hours before serving.

2. Filling: Trim fat from beef. Cut beef into 6 pieces. Place meat in a 3½- or 4-quart slow cooker. Add the undrained canned tomatoes, chipotle chiles, oregano and cumin.

3. Cover slow cooker; cook on low-heat setting for 8 to 10 hours or on high-heat setting for 4 to 5 hours.

4. With slotted spoon, transfer meat and tomatoes to a large bowl; reserve cooking liquid in slow cooker. With two forks, pull meat apart into shreds. Stir enough of the reserved liquid into meat and tomatoes to moisten.

5. Burritos: Spoon meat mixture onto tortillas just below centers. Top with cheese and Pico de Gallo Salsa. Roll up tortillas.

*Note: Serrano, chipotle and other hot chiles contain oils that can burn your skin and eyes. Avoid direct contact with them as much as possible. When working with hot chiles, wear plastic or rubber gloves. If your bare hands do touch chiles, wash your hands well with soap and warm water.

Per burrito: 328 cal., 11 g total fat (4 g sat. fat), 65 mg chol., 969 mg sodium, 24 g carbo., 11 g fiber, 32 g pro.

Canadian Maple-Glazed Pot Roast

Orange peel brightens the flavor of this beef chuck roast that features a trio of fall vegetables: parsnips, acorn squash and onions.

PREP: 20 minutes
COOK: 11 to 12 hours on low-heat setting or 5½ to 6 hours on high-heat setting
MAKES: 8 servings

- 1 boneless beef chuck pot roast (2½ to 3 pounds)
- 1 tablespoon vegetable oil
- 4 medium-size parsnips and/or carrots, cut into 3-inch pieces
- 1 medium-size acorn squash, seeded and cut into 1-inch slices
- 2 small onions, cut into wedges
- ½ cup pure maple syrup or maple-flavored syrup
- 3 tablespoons quick-cooking tapioca
- 2 tablespoons white wine vinegar
- 2 teaspoons finely shredded orange peel
- 1 teaspoon salt
- ¼ teaspoon black pepper
- 4 cups hot cooked noodles

1. Trim fat from beef. If necessary, cut beef to fit into 4- to 5-quart slow cooker. In large skillet, heat oil over medium heat. Brown beef in hot oil, turning to brown on all sides. Drain off fat.

2. In the slow cooker, combine parsnips and/or carrots, acorn squash and onions. Place beef on vegetables. In small bowl, combine maple syrup, tapioca, vinegar, orange peel, salt and pepper. Pour over beef and vegetables in cooker.

3. Cover slow cooker; cook on low-heat setting for 11 to 12 hours or on high-heat setting for 5½ to 6 hours.

4. Transfer beef and vegetables to a serving platter. Skim fat from cooking liquid. Pass cooking liquid with beef. Serve with hot cooked noodles.

Per serving: 423 cal., 8 g total fat (2 g sat. fat), 110 mg chol., 400 mg sodium, 51 g carbo., 4 g fiber, 36 g pro.

Mushroom Steak Diane Stew

The flavors of the classic French dish called Steak Diane—mustard, shallots or onions, and coarse-ground pepper—are translated here into an easy-on-the-cook stew.

PREP: 20 minutes
COOK: 8 to 10 hours on low-heat setting or 4 to 5 hours on high-heat setting
MAKES: 6 servings

- 1½ pounds boneless beef round steak
- 2 medium-size onions, cut into thin wedges
- 3 cups sliced fresh button mushrooms (½ pound)
- 1 can (10¾ ounces) condensed golden mushroom soup
- ¼ cup tomato paste
- 2 teaspoons Worcestershire sauce
- 1 teaspoon dry mustard
- ½ teaspoon cracked black pepper
- 3 cups hot cooked noodles

1. Trim fat from beef. Cut beef into 1-inch pieces; set aside. In 3½- or 4-quart slow cooker, place onions; top with mushrooms. Add beef. In medium-size bowl, stir together mushroom soup, tomato paste, Worcestershire sauce, dry mustard and pepper. Pour over beef mixture in cooker.

2. Cover slow cooker; cook on low-heat setting for 8 to 10 hours or on high-heat setting for 4 to 5 hours. Serve over hot cooked noodles.

Per serving: 335 cal., 9 g total fat (2 g sat. fat), 91 mg chol., 467 mg sodium, 31 g carbo., 3 g fiber, 32 g pro.

Five-Spice Beef Short Ribs

Five-spice powder is an Asian spice blend that most commonly contains fennel, cloves, cinnamon, star anise, and Szechuan peppercorns. Look for it in the spice aisle of your supermarket.

PREP: 25 minutes
COOK: 11 to 12 hours on low-heat setting or 5½ to 6 hours on high-heat setting
MAKES: 8 servings

- 6 **pounds boneless beef short ribs**
- 1 **large red onion, cut into thin wedges (1 cup)**
- 2 **tablespoons quick-cooking tapioca, crushed**
- ⅔ **cup beef broth**
- ¼ **cup soy sauce**
- ¼ **cup rice vinegar**
- 2 **tablespoons honey**
- 1 **tablespoon five-spice powder**
- 1 **teaspoon ground ginger**
- 4 **cloves garlic, minced**
- 4 **cups hot cooked rice**

1. Trim fat from beef. Place onion in 5- to 6-quart slow cooker. Sprinkle with tapioca. Top with beef. In a medium-size bowl, stir together beef broth, soy sauce, vinegar, honey, five-spice powder, ginger and garlic; pour over beef in cooker.

2. Cover slow cooker; cook on low-heat setting for 11 to 12 hours or on high-heat setting for 5½ to 6 hours.

3. With slotted spoon, remove beef and onion from cooker. Pour cooking liquid into a 1-quart glass measuring cup. Skim fat from liquid; discard fat.

4. Serve beef, onion and cooking liquid over cooked rice.

Per serving: 366 cal., 12 g total fat (5 g sat. fat), 79 mg chol., 628 mg sodium, 33 g carbo., 1 g fiber, 30 g pro.

Ranch Pork Roast

Ranch Pork Roast

Add a side of steamed green beans, broccoli or dilled baby carrots to this meat-and-potatoes dish, and you've got a complete meal.

PREP: 15 minutes
COOK: 9 to 10 hours on low-heat setting or 4½ to 5 hours on high-heat setting
MAKES: 6 servings

Nonstick cooking spray
1 **boneless pork shoulder roast (2½ to 3 pounds)**
1 **pound new red-skinned potatoes, halved**
1 **can (10¾ ounces) condensed cream of chicken soup**
1 **package (8 ounces) cream cheese, cubed and softened**
1 **packet (0.4 ounces) dry ranch salad dressing mix**

1. Trim fat from pork. Lightly coat a large skillet with nonstick cooking spray; heat over medium heat. Brown pork on all sides in hot skillet. Remove from heat.

2. Place potatoes in 3½- or 4-quart slow cooker. Place pork on top of potatoes. In medium-size bowl, whisk together soup, cream cheese and salad dressing mix. Spoon soup mixture over pork and potatoes in cooker.

3. Cover slow cooker; cook on low-heat setting for 9 to 10 hours or on high-heat setting for 4½ to 5 hours.

Per serving: 525 cal., 26 g total fat (13 g sat. fat), 159 mg chol., 815 mg sodium, 19 g carbo., 2 g fiber, 41 g pro.

Mushroom-Sauced Pork Chops

Serve this hearty meat dish over hot cooked rice or mashed potatoes—or hot buttered egg noodles.

PREP: 15 minutes
COOK: 8 to 9 hours on low-heat setting or 4 to 4½ hours on high-heat setting
MAKES: 4 servings

     4 pork loin chops, cut ¾ inch thick
     1 tablespoon vegetable oil
     1 small onion, thinly sliced
     2 tablespoons quick-cooking tapioca
     1 can (10¾ ounces) condensed cream of mushroom soup
    ½ cup apple juice
     1 can (4 ounces) sliced mushrooms, drained
     2 teaspoons Worcestershire sauce
    ¾ teaspoon dried thyme
    ¼ teaspoon garlic powder
        Hot cooked rice or mashed potatoes

1. Trim fat from chops. In large skillet, brown chops on both sides in hot oil. In a 3½- or 4-quart slow cooker, place onion; add chops. Crush tapioca with a mortar and pestle. In medium-size bowl, combine tapioca, soup, apple juice, mushrooms, Worcestershire sauce, thyme and garlic powder; pour over chops in cooker.

2. Cover slow cooker; cook on low-heat setting for 8 to 9 hours or on high-heat setting for 4 to 4½ hours. Serve over rice.

For 5- to 6-quart slow cooker: Use 6 pork loin chops, cut ¾ inch thick. Leave remaining ingredient amounts the same and prepare as above. Makes 6 servings.

Per serving: 336 cal., 9 g total fat (2 g sat. fat), 51 mg chol., 517 mg sodium, 39 g carbo., 2 g fiber, 23 g pro.

Sausage Supreme Sandwiches

Use a good cooking apple such as a Granny Smith, Fuji, McIntosh, Newtown Pippin or Jonathan in this German-style dish.

PREP: 20 minutes
COOK: 5 to 6 hours on low-heat setting or 2½ to 3 hours on high-heat setting
MAKES: 6 to 8 sandwiches

     6 to 8 bratwurst or Polish sausage links (about 2 pounds)
     2 large apples, peeled and sliced
     2 cloves garlic, minced
     2 tablespoons packed dark-brown sugar
    ⅛ teaspoon black pepper
    ½ cup apple cider or apple juice
    ¼ cup balsamic vinegar
     1 red onion, thinly sliced
     6 to 8 bratwurst or hot dog buns

1. Place bratwurst in a 3½- or 4-quart slow cooker. Top with apple slices and garlic. Sprinkle with brown sugar and pepper. Pour apple cider and balsamic vinegar over all; top with onion.

2. Cover slow cooker; cook on low-heat setting for 5 to 6 hours or on high-heat setting for 2½ to 3 hours. Serve bratwurst in buns. Use a slotted spoon to top bratwurst with apple and onion.

Per sandwich: 479 cal., 27 g total fat (9 g sat. fat), 63 mg chol., 930 mg sodium, 41 g carbo., 3 g fiber, 16 g pro.

Hot Kielbasa and Potato Salad

This recipe is just-right-sized for two people and a 1½-quart slow cooker.

PREP: 20 minutes
COOK: 6 to 8 hours on low-heat setting or 3½ to 4 hours on high-heat setting
MAKES: 2 servings

- 5   whole tiny new potatoes (about 6 ounces)
- ½   pound cooked turkey kielbasa or smoked sausage, cut into ¾-inch pieces
- 1   rib celery, chopped (½ cup)
- 1   small onion, chopped (⅓ cup)
- ¾   cup water
- ¼   cup cider vinegar
- 2   tablespoons sugar
- 1   tablespoon quick-cooking tapioca
- ¼   teaspoon celery seeds
- ¼   teaspoon black pepper
- 3   cups fresh baby spinach leaves

1. Scrub potatoes with a stiff brush. Cut potatoes into halves or quarters. Place in a 1½-quart slow cooker. Add sausage, celery and onion. In small bowl, stir together the water, vinegar, sugar, tapioca, celery seeds and pepper. Pour over vegetables and sausage.

2. Cover slow cooker. If cooker has heat setting choices, cook on low-heat setting for 6 to 8 hours or on high-heat setting for 3½ to 4 hours. If cooker does not have heat setting choices, cook for 5 to 6 hours.

3. To serve, divide spinach between salad plates. Drizzle about 2 tablespoons of the cooking juices over the spinach on each plate. Stir sausage mixture. With a slotted spoon, remove potatoes, sausage and vegetables from cooker; arrange on top of spinach. Serve immediately.

Per serving: 332 cal., 9 g total fat (0 g sat. fat), 0 mg chol., 1,122 mg sodium, 40 g carbo., 3 g fiber, 24 g pro.

Country-Style Pork Ribs

Serve these meaty ribs with coleslaw and oven-baked sweet potato fries—either homemade or frozen.

PREP: 15 minutes
COOK: 10 to 12 hours on low-heat setting or 5 to 6 hours on high-heat setting plus 10 minutes for sauce
MAKES: 4 to 6 servings

- 1 **large onion, sliced and separated into rings**
- 2½ **to 3 pounds pork country-style ribs**
- 1½ **cups vegetable juice cocktail**
- ½ **of a can (6 ounces) tomato paste (⅓ cup)**
- ¼ **cup molasses**
- 3 **tablespoons vinegar**
- 1 **teaspoon dry mustard**
- ¼ **teaspoon salt**
- ¼ **teaspoon black pepper**
- ⅛ **teaspoon dried thyme**
- ⅛ **teaspoon dried rosemary**

1. Place onion rings in 3½- to 6-quart slow cooker. Place ribs on top of onion. In medium-size bowl, combine vegetable juice cocktail, tomato paste, molasses, vinegar, mustard, salt, pepper, thyme and rosemary. Reserve 1 cup for sauce; cover and refrigerate. Pour remaining juice mixture over ribs in slow cooker.

2. Cover slow cooker; cook on low-heat setting for 10 to 12 hours or on high-heat setting for 5 to 6 hours.

3. For sauce, in small saucepan, bring reserved juice mixture to a boil; reduce heat. Simmer, uncovered, for 10 minutes. Drain ribs; discard cooking liquid. Serve sauce with ribs.

Per serving: 337 cal., 9 g total fat (3 g sat. fat), 117 mg chol., 506 mg sodium, 27 g carbo., 2 g fiber, 36 g pro.

Chicken Cassoulet

The classic French dish called cassoulet is slow cooked in the oven, but making it in a slow cooker renders the same great result: A hearty, satisfying dish perfect for a cold night and a glass of red wine.

PREP: 25 minutes
STAND: 1 hour
COOK: 9 to 11 hours on low-heat setting or 4½ to 5½ hours on high-heat setting
MAKES: 6 servings

- 1 **cup dry navy beans**
- 1 **cup tomato juice**
- 1 **tablespoon Worcestershire sauce**
- 1 **teaspoon instant beef or chicken bouillon granules**
- ½ **teaspoon dried basil**
- ½ **teaspoon dried oregano**
- ½ **teaspoon paprika**
- 1 **medium-size carrot, chopped (½ cup)**
- 1 **rib celery, chopped (½ cup)**
- 1 **medium-size onion, chopped (½ cup)**
- 3 **pounds bone-in chicken thighs and drumsticks, skinned**
- ½ **pound cooked Polish sausage, halved lengthwise and cut into 1-inch pieces**

1. Rinse beans; place in medium-size saucepan. Add enough water to cover beans by 2 inches. Bring to a boil; reduce heat. Simmer, uncovered, for 10 minutes. Remove from heat. Cover; let stand for 1 hour. Drain and rinse beans.

2. In medium-size bowl, combine drained beans, tomato juice, Worcestershire sauce, bouillon granules, basil, oregano and paprika. Set aside.

3. In 3½- or 4-quart slow cooker, combine carrot, celery and onion. Place chicken and sausage on vegetables. Pour bean mixture over chicken and sausage.

4. Cover slow cooker; cook on low-heat setting for 9 to 11 hours or on high-heat setting for 4½ to 5½ hours.

Per serving: 412 cal., 16 g total fat (5 g sat. fat), 130 mg chol., 728 mg sodium, 26 g carbo., 9 g fiber, 39 g pro.

Chicken and Sausage Gumbo

The base of gumbo is roux—a blend of flour and oil that's cooked until it's a coppery color, like that of a tarnished penny. You can actually make the roux a day ahead (it doesn't need to be refrigerated, just stored in a tightly sealed container), then stir everything together the next day.

PREP: 40 minutes
COOK: 6 to 7 hours on low-heat setting or 3 to 3½ hours on high-heat setting
MAKES: 5 servings

- ⅓ **cup all-purpose flour**
- ⅓ **cup vegetable oil**
- 3 **cups water**
- 12 **ounces cooked smoked sausage links, quartered and sliced lengthwise**
- 1½ **cups chopped cooked chicken or 12 ounces boneless, skinless chicken breasts or thighs, cut into ¾-inch pieces**
- 2 **cups sliced okra or 1 package (10 ounces) frozen whole okra, partially thawed and sliced ½ inch thick**
- 1 **large onion, chopped (1 cup)**
- ½ **cup chopped green pepper**
- 1 **rib celery, chopped (½ cup)**
- 4 **cloves garlic, minced**
- ½ **teaspoon salt**
- ½ **teaspoon black pepper**
- ¼ **teaspoon cayenne pepper**
- 3 **cups hot cooked rice**

1. For roux, in heavy, medium-size saucepan, stir together flour and oil until smooth. Cook over medium-high heat for 5 minutes, stirring constantly. Reduce heat to medium. Cook and stir constantly about 15 minutes more or until a dark, reddish brown roux forms. Cool.

2. Pour water into 3½- or 4-quart slow cooker. Stir in roux. Add sausage, chicken, okra, onion, green pepper, celery, garlic, salt, black pepper and cayenne pepper.

3. Cover slow cooker; cook on low-heat setting for 6 to 7 hours or on high-heat setting for 3 to 3½ hours. Skim off fat. Serve over hot cooked rice.

Per serving: 618 cal., 37 g total fat (9 g sat. fat), 79 mg chol., 848 mg sodium, 44 g carbo., 3 g fiber, 26 g pro.

Chicken and Noodles with Vegetables

The drumstick-thigh portion of the chicken is juicy, flavorful and inexpensive. If you can't find whole chicken legs, you can use three drumsticks and three thighs.

PREP: 25 minutes
COOK: 8 to 9 hours on low-heat setting or 4 to 4½ hours on high-heat setting
MAKES: 6 servings

- 4 medium-size carrots, sliced (2 cups)
- 3 medium-size onions, chopped (1½ cups)
- 2 ribs celery, sliced (1 cup)
- 2 tablespoons chopped fresh parsley leaves
- 1 bay leaf
- 3 medium-size chicken legs (drumstick-thigh portion, about 2 pounds total), skinned
- 2 cans (10¾ ounces each) reduced-fat and reduced-sodium condensed cream of chicken soup
- ½ cup water
- 1 teaspoon dried thyme
- ¼ teaspoon black pepper
- 10 ounces dried wide noodles (about 5 cups)
- 1 cup frozen peas
  Salt and black pepper (optional)

1. In 3½- or 4-quart slow cooker, combine carrots, onions, celery, parsley and bay leaf. Place chicken on top of vegetables. In large bowl, stir together soup, water, thyme and ¼ teaspoon pepper. Pour soup mixture over chicken in cooker.

2. Cover slow cooker; cook on low-heat setting for 8 to 9 hours or on high-heat setting for 4 to 4½ hours. Remove chicken from slow cooker; cool slightly. Discard bay leaf.

3. Cook noodles following package directions; drain well. While noodles are cooking, stir frozen peas into mixture in slow cooker. Remove chicken from bones; discard bones. Shred or chop meat; stir into mixture in slow cooker.

4. To serve, spoon chicken mixture over noodles. If desired, season to taste with salt and additional pepper.

Per serving: 406 cal., 7 g total fat (2 g sat. fat), 122 mg chol., 532 mg sodium, 56 g carbo., 5 g fiber, 28 g pro.

Chapter 5

Great Grilling

There's nothing like the smoky flavor that open-flame cooking gives to food. Whether you're looking for a weeknight dinner or a weekend barbecue, there's something here to get fired up about.

Citrus Chicken with Herbs and Spices

Hawaiian Chicken BBQ

Terry Moore of Oaklyn, New Jersey, attributes her first-place win in the 2007 Sports Illustrated Tailgate Nation Cook-Off to the portability of her recipe. "You dump everything into a plastic bag, take it with you, grill it, and then throw the mess away in the bag," she says. Her tailgate-related prizes included a towable grill, portable satellite TV, gasoline-powered blender and a generator.

PREP: 25 minutes
GRILL: 50 to 60 minutes
MAKES: 6 servings

Chicken and Marinade:
- 3 to 4 pounds meaty chicken pieces
- ¼ cup sliced scallions (2)
- ¼ cup pineapple juice
- ¼ cup hoisin sauce
- 3 tablespoons soy sauce
- 2 tablespoons honey
- 2 tablespoons sherry
- 2 tablespoons finely chopped fresh ginger
- 1 tablespoon dark Asian sesame oil
- 2 cloves garlic, minced
- 1 teaspoon sugar
- ½ teaspoon salt

Grilled Pineapple:
- 1 fresh pineapple, peeled, cored and cut into rings
- 2 tablespoons (¼ stick) butter, melted
- ½ cup chopped macadamia nuts, toasted
- ⅓ cup sliced scallions

1. Chicken and Marinade: Put chicken in food-storage bag. In medium-size bowl, combine ¼ cup scallions, pineapple juice, hoisin sauce, soy sauce, honey, sherry, ginger, sesame oil, garlic, sugar and salt. Stir until combined. Pour marinade over the chicken; seal bag. Marinate in the refrigerator for 3 hours, turning bag occasionally. Drain chicken; discard marinade.

2. Heat gas grill to medium-high; adjust grill for indirect cooking. Or prepare charcoal grill with medium-hot coals; arrange coals around drip pan. Test for medium heat above drip pan. Place chicken pieces, bone sides down, on grill rack over drip pan. Cover and grill for 50 to 60 minutes or until internal temperature registers 170° for breast halves and 180° for thighs and drumsticks.

3. Grilled Pineapple: Brush pineapple rings with the melted butter. Add to grill rack over medium coals. Grill for 2 minutes. Turn pineapple rings and grill 2 to 3 minutes more or until lightly browned.

4. Arrange chicken and pineapple rings on a large serving platter. Sprinkle with macadamia nuts and ⅓ cup sliced scallions.

Per serving: 489 cal., 32 g total fat (9 g sat. fat), 140 mg chol., 375 mg sodium, 16 g carbo., 2 g fiber, 34 g pro.

Cajun Beef Southwestern Salad

Michelle Benthin of Gates, Oregon, loves salad and she loves grilling. Her Cajun-spiced grilled beef salad earned her a spot at the 2007 National Beef Cook-Off® in Chicago. "My husband has high cholesterol and I wanted to cook something that is healthy and has a lot of color," she says. "I started adding lots of fruits and vegetables to our diet."

PREP: 30 minutes
BAKE: at 350° for 25 to 35 minutes
GRILL: 8 to 10 minutes
MAKES: 6 servings

12 fresh figs, stems removed, cut into quarters*

Dressing:
3 blood oranges
2 tablespoons extra-virgin olive oil
1½ teaspoons Cajun seasoning

Steak:
3 boneless beef top loin (strip) steaks, cut ¾ inch
    thick (about 1½ pounds total)
1 tablespoon Cajun seasoning

Salad:
9 cups fresh spinach
1 can (15 ounces) garbanzo beans (chickpeas),
    rinsed and drained
1 medium-size red onion, thinly sliced
½ cup coarsely chopped pistachio nuts
½ cup crumbled Gorgonzola or other blue cheese
    (2 ounces)

1. Heat oven to 350°. Place figs, cut sides up, on rimmed baking sheet. Bake at 350° for 25 to 35 minutes or until figs are very soft and start to caramelize.

2. Dressing: Finely shred the peel and squeeze the juice from 1 of the oranges. In small bowl, combine ¼ cup orange juice, orange peel, olive oil and the 1½ teaspoons Cajun seasoning. Set aside. Peel and separate segments from remaining 2 oranges. Set aside.

3. Steak: Heat gas grill to medium or prepare charcoal grill with medium coals. Trim fat from steaks. Press the 1 tablespoon Cajun seasoning evenly onto steaks. Grill steaks for 8 to 10 minutes or until internal temperature registers 145° (medium rare) on an instant-read meat thermometer inserted in center of steaks. Turn steaks over once, halfway through grilling. Let steaks rest for 5 minutes. Slice steaks thinly.

4. Salad: Layer spinach, beans, onion, figs, orange segments and steak slices on a serving platter or on individual plates. Top with nuts and cheese. Drizzle with orange dressing.

*Note: If you cannot find fresh figs, use dried figs. Remove the stems and cut into quarters, but do not bake. Soak in dressing while you prepare the salad.

Per serving: 474 cal., 19 g total fat (5 g sat. fat), 49 mg chol., 589 mg sodium, 50 g carbo., 10 g fiber, 30 g pro.

Cajun Beef Southwestern Salad

Three-Pepper Beef Tenderloin Roast

For a big party and a crowd-pleasing meal, it doesn't get much easier than this nicely spiced and grilled tenderloin roast. It's equally good served warm or at room temperature.

PREP: 15 minutes
GRILL: 1 to 1¼ hours
STAND: 15 minutes
MAKES: 9 or 10 servings

  1 **beef tenderloin roast (3 to 3½ pounds)**
  1 **teaspoon salt**
  1 **teaspoon dried oregano**
  1 **teaspoon dried thyme**
  1 **teaspoon paprika**
  ½ **teaspoon garlic powder**
  ½ **teaspoon onion powder**
  ½ **teaspoon white pepper**
  ½ **teaspoon black pepper**
  ¼ **teaspoon cayenne pepper**

1. Trim fat from roast. In small bowl, combine salt, oregano, thyme, paprika, garlic powder, onion powder, white pepper, black pepper and cayenne pepper. Sprinkle evenly over roast; rub in with your fingers.

2. Heat gas grill to high; reduce heat to medium-high and adjust for indirect cooking. Or prepare charcoal grill with hot coals; arrange coals around drip pan. Test for medium-hot heat above pan. Add additional coals as needed to maintain temperature. Place roast on grill rack over drip pan. (For gas grill, place meat on rack in roasting pan.) Cover and grill for 1 to 1¼ hours or until internal temperature registers 135° (medium rare) when inserted into thickest part of roast.

3. Remove meat from grill; cover with foil and let stand for 15 minutes before carving. (The meat's temperature will rise about 10° during standing.)

Per serving: 252 cal., 13 g total fat (5 g sat. fat), 93 mg chol., 329 mg sodium, 1 g carbo., 0 g fiber, 32 g pro.

Beef Steaks with Gorgonzola Butter

To toast the nuts, spread them out in a single layer and place in a 350° oven until they're golden brown. Watch the pine nuts closely—they burn very easily. They'll toast in about 5 minutes while the walnuts may take a little longer—about 8 to 10 minutes.

PREP: 15 minutes
GRILL: 10 to 12 minutes
MAKES: 4 servings

Gorgonzola Butter:

- 2 tablespoons crumbled Gorgonzola cheese or blue cheese
- 2 tablespoons soft-style cream cheese with onion and garlic or chive and onion
- 1 to 2 tablespoons butter, softened
- 1 tablespoon chopped pine nuts or walnuts, toasted

Steaks:

- 4 boneless beef top loin steaks, cut 1 inch thick (about 3 pounds total)
  Salt

1. Gorgonzola Butter: In small bowl, stir together Gorgonzola cheese, cream cheese, butter and nuts. Shape into a 1-inch-diameter log. Wrap in plastic wrap. Refrigerate until firm.

2. Steaks: Trim fat from steaks. Sprinkle steaks lightly with salt. Heat gas grill to medium or prepare charcoal grill with medium coals. Grill steaks for 10 to 12 minutes or until internal temperature registers 145° (medium rare) on an instant-read meat thermometer inserted in center of steaks. Turn steaks over once, halfway through grilling.

3. To serve, cut butter log into 8 slices. Place 2 slices of butter on each steak; serve immediately.

Per serving: 700 cal., 42 g total fat (18 g sat. fat), 216 mg chol., 429 mg sodium, 1 g carbo., 0 g fiber, 75 g pro.

Peppery Blue Cheese Burgers

There are several brands of Montreal steak seasoning, but most of them contain some blend of garlic, onion, paprika, salt, black pepper, coriander, dill and red pepper flakes or cayenne.

PREP: 25 minutes
GRILL: 20 to 24 minutes
MAKES: 6 burgers

- 2 pounds lean ground beef
- 3 tablespoons Worcestershire sauce
- 3 tablespoons reduced-sodium soy sauce
- 1 tablespoon Cajun seasoning
- 1 tablespoon Montreal steak seasoning
- 1 cup blue cheese, crumbled (4 ounces)
- 12 strips bacon
- ¼ cup finely chopped sweet onion
- 2 cloves garlic, minced
- 3 tablespoons butter, softened
- 3 tablespoons mayonnaise
- 1 teaspoon Dijon mustard
- 6 kaiser rolls or hamburger buns, split and toasted
  Crumbled blue cheese (optional)
  Tomato slices
  Lettuce leaves

1. In large bowl, combine ground beef, Worcestershire sauce, soy sauce, Cajun seasoning and Montreal steak seasoning. Mix well. Gently stir in the 1 cup blue cheese. Shape beef mixture into six ¾-inch-thick patties.

2. Heat gas grill to medium-high; reduce heat to medium and adjust for indirect cooking. Or, prepare charcoal grill with medium-hot coals; arrange coals around a drip pan. Test for medium heat above drip pan. Place patties on grill rack over pan. Cover and grill for 20 to 24 minutes or until internal temperature registers 160° on an instant-read meat thermometer inserted in centers of patties. Turn patties over once halfway through grilling.

3. In large skillet, cook bacon over medium heat until crisp, turning occasionally. Drain on paper towels. Drain skillet, reserving 1 tablespoon drippings. Cook onion and garlic in reserved drippings over medium heat for 3 to 5 minutes or until tender, stirring occasionally. Remove from heat and cool slightly. In small bowl, combine butter, mayonnaise, mustard and cooked onion mixture.

4. Place burgers on roll bottoms. If desired, top with additional blue cheese. Add bacon, tomato slices, lettuce leaves and the mayonnaise mixture. Replace roll tops.

Per burger: 791 cal., 51 g total fat (20 g sat. fat), 155 mg chol., 1,952 mg sodium, 36 g carbo., 2 g fiber, 45 g pro.

Grilled Steak Bruschetta Salad

You can use toasted slices of baguette as a base for the meat, peppers and cheese—or toasted slices of ciabatta. Ciabatta (chah-bah-ta) is a wonderfully hearty, chewy bread whose name means slipper in Italian for its long, flat shape.

PREP: 25 minutes
GRILL: 10 to 15 minutes
MAKES: 4 servings

Apricot Dressing:
- ¼ **cup apricot preserves**
- ¼ **cup prepared horseradish**
- ¼ **cup creamy Dijon mustard blend**
- 2 **tablespoons lemon juice**

Steak and Bruschetta:
- 4 **beef tenderloin steaks, cut 1 inch thick (about 1½ pounds total)**
- ¼ **teaspoon salt**
- ¼ **teaspoon black pepper**
- 12 **¼-inch-thick slices baguette-style French bread**

Salad:
- 4 **cups arugula**
- ¼ **cup bottled roasted sweet red peppers, chopped**
- ¼ **cup crumbled blue cheese**

1. Apricot Dressing: With kitchen scissors, snip any large pieces in preserves. In small bowl, combine preserves, horseradish, mustard blend and lemon juice. Set aside.

2. Steak and Bruschetta: Sprinkle steaks on both sides with salt and pepper. Heat gas grill to medium or prepare charcoal grill with medium coals. Grill steaks for 10 to 15 minutes or until internal temperature registers 145° (medium rare) on an instant-read meat thermometer. Turn steaks over once halfway through grilling. Grill bread slices with steaks during last 2 minutes, until toasted; turn once.

3. Salad: Divide arugula among 4 serving plates. Top with bread slices. Drizzle with Apricot Dressing. Slice steak; arrange on bread. Top with roasted peppers and blue cheese.

Per serving: 488 cal., 17 g total fat (7 g sat. fat), 111 mg chol., 964 mg sodium, 39 g carbo., 2 g fiber, 43 g pro.

Glazed Country Ribs

Glazed Country Ribs

Brushing the sauce on the ribs just the last 10 minutes of cooking time keeps it from burning. It only needs a few minutes to get hot and form a nice, saucy crust on the meat.

PREP: 15 minutes
GRILL: $1\frac{1}{2}$ to 2 hours
MAKES: 4 servings

1	**cup ketchup**
$\frac{1}{2}$	**cup water**
$\frac{1}{4}$	**cup finely chopped onion**
$\frac{1}{4}$	**cup cider vinegar or wine vinegar**
$\frac{1}{4}$	**cup mild-flavored molasses**
2	**tablespoons Worcestershire sauce**
2	**teaspoons chili powder**
2	**cloves garlic, minced**
$2\frac{1}{2}$	**to 3 pounds pork country-style ribs**

1. In medium-size saucepan, combine ketchup, water, onion, vinegar, molasses, Worcestershire sauce, chili powder and garlic. Bring to a boil; reduce heat. Simmer, uncovered, for 10 to 15 minutes or to desired consistency, stirring often.

2. Trim fat from ribs. Heat gas grill to medium-high and adjust for indirect cooking. Or, prepare charcoal grill with medium-hot coals; arrange coals around drip pan. Test for medium heat above drip pan. Add additional coals as necessary to maintain heat. Place ribs, bone sides down, on grill rack over drip pan. (Or, place ribs in a rib rack; place on grill rack.) Cover and grill for $1\frac{1}{2}$ to 2 hours or until tender, brushing occasionally with sauce during the last 10 minutes of grilling. Pass remaining sauce with ribs.

Per serving: 527 cal., 24 g total fat (9 g sat. fat), 148 mg chol., 821 mg sodium, 34 g carbo., 1 g fiber, 44 g pro.

Pork Tenderloin with Blackberry Sauce

A sweet and fruity blackberry sauce is a delicious complement to the savory marinated meat.

PREP: 40 minutes
MARINATE: 2 to 4 hours
GRILL: 30 to 45 minutes
COOK: 10 minutes
MAKES: 4 servings

Pork and Marinade:
- 1 pork tenderloin (1 pound)
- 1/3 cup dry white wine
- 1/4 cup olive oil
- 3 tablespoons balsamic vinegar
- 2 tablespoons Dijon mustard
- 1/2 teaspoon soy sauce
- 2 cloves garlic, minced
- 1 teaspoon chopped fresh rosemary
- 1/4 teaspoon black pepper
- Dash cayenne pepper

Blackberry Sauce:
- 1/4 cup seedless blackberry jam
- 1 teaspoon finely shredded lemon peel

1. Pork and Marinade: Place pork in food-storage bag set in shallow dish. Combine remaining marinade ingredients. Pour over pork; seal bag. Marinate in refrigerator 2 to 4 hours. Drain, reserving marinade.

2. Heat gas grill to medium-high; reduce heat to medium and adjust for indirect cooking. Or prepare charcoal grill with medium-hot coals; arrange coals around drip pan. Place pork on grill over drip pan. Cover and grill 30 to 45 minutes or until internal temperature registers 155° on an instant-read thermometer. Remove from grill. Cover with foil; let stand 10 minutes.

3. Blackberry Sauce: In small saucepan, bring reserved marinade to a boil; reduce heat. Simmer, uncovered for 8 to 10 minutes or until reduced by about half. Strain mixture. Return strained mixture to saucepan. Stir in blackberry jam and lemon peel; heat through.

4. Slice pork; arrange on a platter and top with sauce.

Per serving: 339 cal., 16 g total fat (3 g sat. fat), 73 mg chol., 269 mg sodium, 18 g carbo., 0 g fiber, 24 g pro.

Island Glazed Lamb Chops

Lamb loin chops are thicker and meatier than lamb rib chops. They're also the most tender chops on the animal. They're best prepared broiled or grilled, as they are here.

PREP: 15 minutes
COOK: 15 minutes
GRILL: 12 to 14 minutes
MAKES: 4 servings

- 1 cup ketchup
- 1/3 cup molasses
- 1/3 cup cider vinegar
- 1/3 cup dark rum
- 2 tablespoons yellow mustard
- 1 tablespoon Worcestershire sauce
- Several dashes hot-pepper sauce
- 8 lamb loin chops, cut 1 inch thick
- Salt and black pepper

1. In small saucepan, combine ketchup, molasses, vinegar, rum, mustard, Worcestershire sauce and hot-pepper sauce. Bring to a boil; reduce heat. Simmer, uncovered, for 15 to 20 minutes or until desired consistency, stirring occasionally.

2. Trim fat from chops. Sprinkle chops with salt and pepper. Heat gas grill to medium or prepare charcoal grill with medium coals. Grill chops for 12 to 14 minutes or until internal temperature registers 145° (medium rare) on an instant-read meat thermometer inserted in center of chops. Turn chops over once halfway through grilling and brush with ketchup mixture during the last 5 minutes of grilling.

3. Reheat and pass remaining ketchup mixture.

Per serving: 386 cal., 8 g total fat (3 g sat. fat), 90 mg chol., 1,035 mg sodium, 38 g carbo., 1 g fiber, 30 g pro.

Rosemary Lamb Chops

Greeks, Italians—most Mediterraneans, really—love lamb. These meaty chops are infused with the flavors of that region: red wine, rosemary, balsamic vinegar and garlic.

PREP: 35 minutes
GRILL: 12 to 14 minutes
MARINATE: 2 to 24 hours
MAKES: 4 servings

- 2 to 2¼ pounds lamb rib chops
- ¾ cup dry red wine
- 3 tablespoons chopped fresh rosemary
- 1 tablespoon balsamic vinegar
- 2 cloves garlic, minced
- ½ teaspoon coarsely ground black pepper
- ¼ teaspoon salt
- 1 tablespoon butter
- Parsley mashed potatoes, for serving (optional)

1. Trim fat from chops. Place chops in food-storage bag set in shallow dish. Add wine, 2 tablespoons of the rosemary, the vinegar, garlic, pepper and salt to the bag. Seal bag. Marinate in the refrigerator for at least 2 hours or up to 24 hours, turning bag occasionally. Drain chops, reserving marinade.

2. Heat gas grill to medium or prepare charcoal grill with medium coals. Grill lamb chops for 12 to 14 minutes or until internal temperature registers 145° (medium rare) on an instant-read meat thermometer inserted in centers of chops. Turn chops once, halfway through grilling.

3. Strain reserved marinade into small saucepan; discard solids. Bring marinade to a boil; reduce heat. Simmer, uncovered, about 5 minutes or until reduced to about ⅓ cup. Add butter and the remaining 1 tablespoon rosemary; cook for 1 minute. Serve with the chops. If desired, serve with parsley mashed potatoes.

Per serving: 231 cal., 11 g total fat (5 g sat. fat), 71 mg chol., 227 mg sodium, 4 g carbo., 0 g fiber, 20 g pro.

Grilled Chicken Salad

Grilled Chicken Salad

The addition of marinated grilled chicken to a Greek-style salad turns a vegetable side dish into a one-dish meal. Serve it with warm pita bread.

PREP: 30 minutes
MARINATE: 4 to 24 hours
GRILL: 12 to 15 minutes
MAKES: 4 servings

Chicken and Marinade:

- 4 boneless, skinless chicken breast halves (about 1¼ pounds total)
- 1 tablespoon lemon juice
- 1 tablespoon olive oil
- 1 tablespoon chopped fresh oregano leaves or 1 teaspoon dried oregano
- ¼ teaspoon black pepper
- 2 cloves garlic, minced

Salad:

- 3 medium-size cucumbers, seeded and cut into ½-inch pieces
- 2 medium-size tomatoes, cut into ½-inch pieces
- 1 medium-size red onion, chopped (½ cup)
  Mixed salad greens (optional)
- ⅓ cup bottled reduced-calorie ranch or creamy cucumber salad dressing
- ½ cup crumbled feta cheese (2 ounces)
- ¼ cup chopped pitted kalamata olives or ripe olives

1. Chicken and Marinade: Place chicken in food-storage bag set in a shallow dish. For marinade, in small bowl, combine lemon juice, olive oil, oregano, pepper and garlic. Pour over chicken in bag; seal bag. Marinate in the refrigerator for at least 4 hours or up to 24 hours, turning bag occasionally. Drain chicken; discard marinade.

2. Heat gas grill to medium or prepare charcoal grill with medium coals. Grill chicken for 12 to 15 minutes or until temperature registers 170° on an instant-read meat thermometer inserted in chicken. Turn chicken once, halfway through grilling. Transfer chicken to a cutting board; cut into bite-size pieces.

3. Salad: In medium-size bowl, toss together cucumbers, tomatoes and red onion. Add chicken; toss to mix. If desired, serve on greens. Drizzle dressing over salad. Sprinkle with feta cheese and olives.

Per serving: 330 cal., 12 g total fat (3 g sat. fat), 95 mg chol., 646 mg sodium, 17 g carbo., 3 g fiber, 37 g pro.

Citrus Chicken with Herbs and Spices

There is no substitute for grinding your own spices, fresh, in a mortar and pestle or spice grinder. Toasting them first intensifies their flavors and wonderful aromas even more.

PREP: 25 minutes
MARINATE: 4 to 8 hours
GRILL: 50 to 60 minutes
MAKES: 6 servings

- 1 **teaspoon coriander seeds**
- 1 **teaspoon fennel seeds**
- 2½ **to 3 pounds meaty chicken pieces**
- ½ **cup orange juice**
- ¼ **cup thinly sliced scallions (2)**
- 3 **tablespoons honey**
- 1 **tablespoon chopped fresh thyme leaves**
- 1 **tablespoon chopped fresh sage leaves**
- 1 **tablespoon chopped fresh rosemary**
- ½ **teaspoon salt**
- ½ **teaspoon cracked black pepper**
  Sautéed snow peas and cherry tomatoes, for serving (optional)

1. In small skillet, cook coriander seeds and fennel seeds over medium heat about 5 minutes or until seeds are fragrant and toasted, stirring constantly. Remove from heat; let cool. Crush seeds with mortar and pestle.

2. If desired, remove skin from chicken. Place chicken in food-storage bag set in shallow dish. In small bowl, combine orange juice, scallions, honey, thyme, sage, rosemary, salt and pepper. Stir in crushed seeds. Pour over chicken; seal bag. Marinate in the refrigerator for 4 to 8 hours, turning bag occasionally. Drain chicken, discarding marinade.

3. Heat gas grill to medium-high; adjust grill for indirect cooking. Or prepare charcoal grill with medium-hot coals; arrange coals around drip pan. Place chicken pieces, bone sides down, over drip pan. Cover; grill for 50 to 60 minutes or until temperature registers 170° for breast halves and 180° for thighs and drumsticks. If desired, serve with snow peas and cherry tomatoes.

Per serving: 260 cal., 11 g total fat (3 g sat. fat), 86 mg chol., 272 mg sodium, 12 g carbo., 1 g fiber, 28 g pro.

Onion-Parmesan Turkey Burgers

When cooked directly on the grill rack, these turkey burgers stick and fall apart, but on the foil they hold their shape, pick up plenty of smoky flavor and even get great grill marks.

PREP: 20 minutes
GRILL: 14 to 16 minutes
MAKES: 8 burgers

1½ **cups chopped onions (3 medium-size)**
1 **tablespoon olive oil**
¼ **cup dry white wine**
1 **cup seasoned stuffing croutons**
1 **egg**
1 **teaspoon Dijon mustard**
½ **teaspoon salt**
2 **pounds uncooked ground turkey**
1 **cup grated Parmesan cheese**
8 **ciabatta rolls, split and toasted**
½ **cup bottled Caesar or ranch salad dressing**
8 **tomato slices**
8 **large fresh basil leaves**

1. In large skillet, cook onion in hot olive oil until tender. Carefully add wine; cook about 8 minutes or until liquid is evaporated and onions are golden. Cool slightly.

2. Place stuffing croutons in food processor or blender; cover and process or blend until fine crumbs form. Add cooked onion, egg, mustard and salt. Cover and process or blend until smooth. In large bowl, combine turkey and onion mixture. Add Parmesan cheese; mix well. Shape turkey mixture into eight ½-inch-thick patties.

3. Heat gas grill to medium or prepare charcoal grill with medium coals. Place a large piece of nonstick foil (or foil coated with nonstick cooking spray) on grill rack over coals. Place turkey patties on foil. Cover and grill for 14 to 16 minutes or until internal temperature registers 165° on an instant-read meat thermometer inserted in center of patties. Turn patties over once, halfway through grilling.

4. Spread cut sides of rolls with salad dressing. Serve burgers in rolls with tomato slices and basil.

Per burger: 515 cal., 26 g total fat (7 g sat. fat), 125 mg chol., 983 mg sodium, 37 g carbo., 3 g fiber, 31 g pro.

Thai Shrimp Kabobs

A squeeze of fresh lime brightens this rich, coconut-curried shrimp dish. There are several brands of bottled Thai-style green curry paste—all of which pack a wallop. You can add or subtract a little of the paste according to your taste.

PREP: 20 minutes
MARINATE: 30 minutes
GRILL: 5 to 8 minutes
MAKES: 4 to 6 servings

  1 **can (13½ or 14 ounces) unsweetened coconut milk**
1½ **teaspoons finely shredded lime peel**
  3 **tablespoons lime juice**
1½ **teaspoons sugar**
1½ **teaspoons green curry paste**
1½ **teaspoons fish sauce**
  1 **teaspoon grated fresh ginger**
  1 **pound peeled and deveined large shrimp (about 26 to 30)**
  2 **to 3 cups hot cooked rice**
     Lime wedges, for garnish (optional)

1. If using wooden skewers, soak in water for 30 minutes. In small bowl, stir together coconut milk, lime peel, lime juice, sugar, curry paste, fish sauce and fresh ginger.

2. Place shrimp in medium-size bowl. Pour ½ cup of the coconut milk mixture over shrimp. Cover shrimp and refrigerate for 30 minutes. Cover and refrigerate remaining coconut milk mixture.

3. Drain shrimp; discard marinade. Thread shrimp onto metal or wooden skewers, leaving ¼ inch between pieces.

4. Heat gas grill to medium or prepare charcoal grill with medium coals. Grill skewers for 5 to 8 minutes or until shrimp turn pink and are cooked through. Turn skewers over once, halfway through grilling.

5. In medium-size saucepan, bring reserved coconut milk mixture to a boil over medium heat; reduce heat. Simmer, uncovered, for 5 minutes (mixture will be thin). Serve shrimp with rice and warm coconut milk mixture. If desired, garnish with lime wedges.

Per serving: 420 cal., 21 g total fat (16 g sat. fat), 172 mg chol., 350 mg sodium, 30 g carbo., 0 g fiber, 27 g pro.

Salmon with Asian Glaze and Pineapple Rice

To save time, look for fresh, already peeled and cored pineapple in the produce section—or buy a small amount of fresh pineapple from the supermarket salad bar.

PREP: 20 minutes
COOK: 18 minutes
GRILL: 8 to 12 minutes
MAKES: 4 servings

Pineapple Rice:
- 1 **cup chicken broth**
- ¾ **cup jasmine or long-grain rice**
- ½ **cup pineapple juice**
- 1 **cup frozen shelled green or sweet soybeans (edamame)**
- ½ **cup sliced scallions (4)**
- 1 **cup bite-size pieces fresh, peeled pineapple**

Salmon and Asian Glaze:
- 2 **tablespoons hoisin sauce**
- 1 **tablespoon soy sauce**
- 1½ **teaspoons peanut oil**
- 1 **teaspoon grated fresh ginger**
- 1 **clove garlic, minced**
- 4 **fresh skinless salmon fillets (4 ounces each, 1 inch thick)**

1. Pineapple Rice: In medium-size saucepan, combine chicken broth, rice and pineapple juice. Bring to a boil; reduce heat. Cover and simmer for 15 minutes. Stir in soybeans and scallions. Cook about 3 minutes more or until rice is tender. Stir in pineapple. Cover rice and keep warm.

2. Salmon and Asian Glaze: In small bowl, stir together hoisin sauce, soy sauce, peanut oil, ginger and garlic; set aside. Rinse salmon; pat dry with paper towels. Heat gas grill to medium or prepare charcoal grill with medium coals. Grill fish for 8 to 12 minutes or until fish flakes when tested with a fork. Turn fish over once halfway through grilling and brush with glaze during the last 2 minutes of grilling.

3. Serve salmon with Pineapple Rice.

Per serving: 507 cal., 19 g total fat (3 g sat. fat), 68 mg chol., 656 mg sodium, 48 g carbo., 4 g fiber, 35 g pro.

Tuscan Tuna Steaks

All parts of the licoricey-tasting fennel bulb can be eaten—the crisp bulb as a vegetable, and the feathery leaves (called fronds) as an herb or garnish.

PREP: 15 minutes
COOK: 8 minutes
GRILL: 8 to 12 minutes
MAKES: 4 servings

- 4 fresh or frozen tuna steaks (6 ounces each, cut 1 inch thick)
- 1/2 teaspoon salt
- 1/4 teaspoon lemon-pepper seasoning
- 4 teaspoons olive oil
- 1 small bulb fennel
- 2 cloves garlic, minced
- 1/3 cup lemon juice
- 1/4 cup oil-packed dried tomatoes, drained and chopped
- 2 tablespoons crumbled goat cheese (optional)
  Cooked brown rice (optional)

1. Thaw tuna, if frozen. Rinse tuna; pat dry with paper towels. Sprinkle salt and lemon-pepper seasoning over tuna; drizzle with 2 teaspoons of the olive oil. Set aside.

2. Cut off and discard upper stalks of fennel, reserving feathery leaves. Snip enough of the leaves to equal 2 tablespoons; discard remaining leaves. Remove any wilted outer layers from fennel bulb; cut off a thin slice from fennel base. Cut the bulb into 1-inch slices.

3. In medium-size skillet, cook fennel and garlic in the remaining 2 teaspoons hot olive oil over medium-high heat about 5 minutes or until tender. Stir in lemon juice, tomatoes and fennel leaves. Simmer for 3 to 5 minutes or until liquid is slightly thickened and bubbly. Remove skillet from heat; set aside.

4. Grease grill rack or coat with nonstick cooking spray. Heat gas grill to medium or prepare charcoal grill with medium coals. Grill tuna for 8 to 12 minutes or until tuna is slightly pink in center. Turn tuna over once, halfway through grilling.

5. To serve, top tuna with fennel mixture. If desired, sprinkle with goat cheese and serve with brown rice.

Per serving: 337 cal., 15 g total fat (4 g sat. fat), 67 mg chol., 395 mg sodium, 8 g carbo., 2 g fiber, 42 g pro.

Chapter 6

Good For You

Healthful food that's low in fat and calories and high in nutrition- and fiber-rich fruits, vegetables and grains can taste great and easily tempt you to the table. The proof is right here.

Turkey Piccata with Fettuccine

Italian-Style Barley Salad

When Lesley Pew of Lynn, Massachusetts, is going to eat carbohydrates, she goes with the grain. Her first-place-winning entry in the 2008 National Barley Cook-Off was a light, fresh salad based on a recipe for tabbouleh—the Middle-Eastern salad made with bulgur, tomatoes, garlic, lemon and parsley. Make it with ripe summer tomatoes and serve it alongside grilled meats.

PREP: 30 minutes
COOK: 45 minutes
MAKES: 6 to 8 servings

  3 **cups water**
  ¼ **teaspoon salt**
  ¾ **cup regular barley**
  2 **medium-size tomatoes, seeded and chopped (1 cup)**
1½ **cups chopped fresh parsley leaves (about 1 bunch)**
  ½ **cup finely chopped shallots**
  ½ **cup bottled clear Italian salad dressing**
  ½ **cup grated Parmesan cheese**
     Sliced scallions, for garnish

1. In large saucepan, bring water and salt to a boil. Add barley; return to a boil. Reduce heat. Cover and simmer about 45 minutes or until barley is tender. Drain barley, if necessary. Rinse barley with cold water to cool quickly. Drain well.

2. In large bowl, combine cooled barley, tomatoes, parsley, shallots and salad dressing. Serve immediately or cover and refrigerate for up to 24 hours. If chilled, let stand at room temperature for 15 to 20 minutes before serving. Sprinkle with cheese and garnish with scallions before serving.

Per serving: 190 cal., 8 g total fat (2 g sat. fat), 6 mg chol., 542 mg sodium, 24 g carbo., 5 g fiber, 7 g pro.

Mama's Lalapalooza Chili

KatiAnn Watson lives in lentil country around Colfax, Washington—also known as The Palouse, for the Palus tribe that inhabited the area. The "lalapalooza" in the name of her second-place 2008 National Lentil Festival Cook-Off recipe is a play on that. "It means something great and wonderful," she says, "so I thought the chili should have that name."

PREP: 20 minutes
COOK: 65 to 85 minutes
STAND: 10 minutes
MAKES: 8 to 10 servings

- 4 cans (14 ounces each) vegetable broth or 6½ cups water
- 2 cups dry lentils
- 12 ounces uncooked ground turkey
- 1 tablespoon vegetable oil
- 2 tablespoons Spike® All-Natural Seasoning or all-purpose seasoning of choice
- ½ to 1½ teaspoons salt
- ¼ teaspoon black pepper
- 3 ribs celery, chopped (1½ cups)
- 1 large onion, chopped (1 cup)
- 1 tablespoon grapeseed or olive oil
- ½ to 1½ teaspoons red pepper flakes
- 5 large cloves garlic, minced
- 3 tablespoons medium chili powder
- 1 can (14½ ounces) diced tomatoes
- 1 cup purchased medium salsa
- 1½ cups shredded Asiago cheese (6 ounces)
  Finely chopped fresh jalapeño or other hot chile (optional)
  Sour cream, chopped fresh chives and toasted bread, for serving (optional)

1. In 4- to 5-quart Dutch oven, combine vegetable broth or water and lentils. Bring to a boil; reduce heat. Cover and simmer 30 to 40 minutes or until lentils are tender.

2. While lentils are cooking, in large skillet, cook turkey in hot vegetable oil over medium heat about 6 minutes or until browned, stirring occasionally. Stir in seasoning, salt and black pepper. Cook for 2 minutes more, stirring occasionally. Remove turkey from skillet; set aside.

3. In the same skillet, cook celery and onion in hot grapeseed oil over medium heat until translucent and slightly soft, stirring occasionally. Reduce heat to low. Add red pepper flakes; cook and stir for 2 minutes. Add garlic; cook and stir for 2 minutes. Add chili powder; cook and stir for 2 minutes.

4. Add cooked turkey mixture, onion mixture, undrained tomatoes and salsa to lentil mixture in Dutch oven. Return to a boil; reduce heat. Simmer, uncovered, for 35 to 45 minutes or until thick and saucy. (Add a little water, if necessary, to keep chili from becoming too thick or scorching.)

5. Remove from the heat; stir in cheese. Let stand for 10 minutes. If desired, stir in chiles for additional heat. If desired, top servings with sour cream and chives and serve with toasted bread.

Per serving: 403 cal., 15 g total fat (6 g sat. fat), 57 mg chol., 2,662 mg sodium, 42 g carbo., 18 g fiber, 27 g pro.

Mama's Lalapalooza Chili

Flank Steak Teriyaki

Flank steak is among the leanest, most flavorful cuts of beef. It takes very nicely to a teriyaki-style treatment. Serve it with hot cooked rice and colorful sliced bell peppers stir-fried in a little sesame oil.

PREP: 20 minutes
MARINATE: 4 to 24 hours
BROIL: 15 to 18 minutes
MAKES: 4 servings

- 1 pound beef flank steak
- ¼ cup reduced-sodium soy sauce
- 3 tablespoons dry sherry or reduced-sodium beef broth
- 2 tablespoons olive oil
- ¼ cup chopped scallions (2)
- ¼ teaspoon ground ginger
- ⅛ teaspoon black pepper
- 1 clove garlic, minced
  Hot cooked brown rice (optional)

1. Score both sides of steak in a diamond pattern by making shallow diagonal cuts at 1-inch intervals. Place steak in food-storage bag set in a shallow dish. In small bowl, combine soy sauce, sherry, olive oil, scallions, ginger, pepper and garlic. Pour marinade over steak in bag; seal bag. Marinate in the refrigerator for at least 4 hours or up to 24 hours, turning bag occasionally.

2. Preheat broiler. Drain steak; discard marinade. Pat steak dry with paper towels. Place steak on the unheated rack of a broiler pan. Broil 3 to 4 inches from the heat for 15 to 18 minutes or until internal temperature registers 160° (medium) on instant-read meat thermometer inserted in center of steak. Turn steak over once, halfway through broiling. To serve, slice steak thinly across the grain. If desired, serve with rice.

Per serving: 209 cal., 10 g total fat (3 g sat. fat), 47 mg chol., 343 mg sodium, 1 g carbo., 0 g fiber, 25 g pro.

Chicken Teriyaki: Prepare as above, except substitute 4 boneless, skinless chicken breast halves for the flank steak. Broil 4 to 5 inches from the heat for 12 to 15 minutes or until temperature registers 170° on instant-read meat thermometer when inserted in chicken. Turn chicken over once, halfway through broiling.

Spaghetti Pie

Trying to get the kids to eat healthier? This fun, spaghetti-crusted pie will be a hit, guaranteed.

PREP: 30 minutes
BAKE: at 350° for 20 to 25 minutes
MAKES: 6 servings

- 4 ounces spaghetti
- 8 ounces lean ground beef
- 1 medium-size onion, chopped (½ cup)
- ½ cup chopped green pepper
- 1 clove garlic, minced
- ½ teaspoon fennel seeds, crushed
- 1 can (8 ounces) tomato sauce
- 1 teaspoon dried oregano
- 1 tablespoon butter
- 1 egg, lightly beaten
- ¼ cup grated Parmesan cheese
  Nonstick cooking spray
- 1 cup low-fat cottage cheese
- ½ cup shredded part-skim mozzarella cheese (4 ounces)

1. Heat oven to 350°. In large saucepan, cook spaghetti following package directions; drain well. Return spaghetti to saucepan.

2. While spaghetti is cooking, in medium-size skillet, cook ground beef, onion, green pepper, garlic and fennel seeds until meat is brown and onion is tender. Drain off fat. Stir in tomato sauce and oregano; heat through.

3. Toss butter with hot spaghetti until melted. Add egg and Parmesan cheese; toss until well mixed.

4. Coat 9-inch pie plate with nonstick cooking spray. Press spaghetti mixture onto bottom and up sides of pie plate, forming a crust. Spread cottage cheese on bottom and up sides of crust. Spread meat mixture over cottage cheese. Sprinkle with shredded mozzarella cheese.

5. Bake, uncovered, at 350° for 20 to 25 minutes or until heated through. Serve in wedges.

Per serving: 273 cal., 12 g total fat (6 g sat. fat), 78 mg chol., 487 mg sodium, 20 g carbo., 2 g fiber, 20 g pro.

Tex-Mex Pork and Corn Soup

A colorful bowl of this south-of-the-border-style soup will cure whatever ails you—even if that's only hunger. The chipotle-style salsa adds a subtle smoky flavor, but you can really use any kind of salsa you like.

START TO FINISH: 35 minutes
MAKES: 5 servings

- 1 pork tenderloin (12 ounces) or 12 ounces lean boneless pork, cut into bite-size strips
- 1 tablespoon olive oil
- 1 large red onion, chopped (1 cup)
- 4 cloves garlic, minced
- 1 package (10 ounces) frozen whole kernel corn
- 2 cans (14 ounces each) reduced-sodium chicken broth
- 1 cup chipotle-style salsa or regular salsa
- 1 cup chopped sweet red and/or yellow pepper (1 large)
- ¼ cup chopped fresh cilantro leaves
- 1 medium-size tomato, chopped (½ cup)
    Light sour cream, for serving (optional)

1. In large saucepan, cook and stir pork strips in hot oil over medium-high heat for 4 to 5 minutes or until no pink remains. Remove pork strips from saucepan; set aside. Add onion and garlic to saucepan. Cook and stir for 3 to 4 minutes or until onion is tender.

2. Add corn to saucepan. Cook and stir for 4 minutes. Stir in broth, salsa and sweet pepper. Bring to a boil; reduce heat. Simmer, uncovered, for 10 minutes. Return pork strips to saucepan; heat through. Remove saucepan from heat; stir in cilantro. Top each serving with tomato and, if desired, sour cream.

Per serving: 199 cal., 6 g total fat (1 g sat. fat), 44 mg chol., 561 mg sodium, 20 g carbo., 3 g fiber, 19 g pro.

Tex-Mex Chicken and Corn Soup: Prepare as above, except substitute boneless, skinless chicken breast halves, cut into 1-inch pieces, for the pork.

Festive Pork Roast

Festive Pork Roast

You can't beat the ease of this beautiful roast for feeding a big holiday crowd. One flavorful marinade does triple duty—as a marinade, a glaze, and finally, a sauce for serving.

PREP: 15 minutes
MARINATE: 6 to 24 hours
ROAST: at 325° for 1¼ to 1½ hours
STAND: 15 minutes
MAKES: 8 to 10 servings

- 1   **boneless pork top loin roast (single loin, 3 pounds)**
- ¾   **cup dry red wine**
- ⅓   **cup packed brown sugar**
- ¼   **cup vinegar**
- ¼   **cup ketchup**
- ¼   **cup water**
- 1   **tablespoon vegetable oil**
- 1   **tablespoon soy sauce**
- 1   **clove garlic, minced**
- 1   **teaspoon curry powder**
- ½   **teaspoon ground ginger**
- ¼   **teaspoon black pepper**
- 2   **teaspoons cornstarch**

1. Place roast in food storage bag set in a large, deep bowl. In small bowl, combine wine, brown sugar, vinegar, ketchup, water, oil, soy sauce, garlic, curry powder, ginger and pepper. Pour over meat; seal bag. Marinate in the refrigerator for at least 6 hours or up to 24 hours, turning bag several times. Drain meat, reserving 1¼ cups marinade; cover marinade and refrigerate. Pat meat dry with paper towels.

2. Heat oven to 325°. Place the meat on a rack in a shallow roasting pan. Insert an oven-going meat thermometer into center of roast. Roast at 325° for 1¼ to 1½ hours or until meat thermometer registers 150°.

3. While pork is roasting, in small saucepan, stir reserved marinade into the cornstarch. Cook and stir until thickened and bubbly. Cook and stir for 2 minutes more. Brush pork roast frequently with sauce after 1 hour of roasting.

4. Cover meat with foil and let stand for 15 minutes. (The roast's temperature will rise about 10° during standing.) To serve, slice meat. Bring remaining sauce to a boil and pass with meat.

Double-Loin Festive Pork Roast: Prepare as above, except use a 5-pound boneless pork top loin roast (double loin, tied) and double the marinade mixture. Reserve 2½ cups marinade for sauce and increase cornstarch to 4 teaspoons. Roast pork at 325° for 2 to 2½ hours or until thermometer registers 150°. Let stand and serve as above. Makes 15 servings.

Per 4 ounces pork + about 2 tablespoons sauce: 327 cal., 11 g total fat (4 g sat. fat), 93 mg chol., 265 mg sodium, 12 g carbo., 0 g fiber, 38 g pro.

Baked Sausage and Mushroom Rotini

This simple pasta bake doesn't compromise great taste for healthfulness. High-fiber whole-grain pasta and Italian-style turkey sausage stand in for the more traditional—but less healthful—ingredients.

PREP: 40 minutes
BAKE: at 350° about 30 minutes
MAKES: 6 servings

3½   **cups whole-grain rotini or penne**
12   **ounces uncooked turkey Italian sausage links, casings removed; uncooked ground turkey or lean ground beef**
1   **package (8 ounces) sliced fresh mushrooms**
1   **medium-size onion, chopped (½ cup)**
2   **cloves garlic, minced**
2   **cans (14½ ounces each) diced tomatoes with basil, garlic and oregano**
1   **can (6 ounces) no-salt-added tomato paste**
⅓   **cup water**
¼   **teaspoon red pepper flakes**
¼   **cup shredded part-skim mozzarella cheese (1 ounce)**
¼   **cup freshly grated Parmesan cheese (1 ounce)**

1. Heat oven to 350°. Cook pasta following package directions; drain well.

2. While pasta is cooking, in 4-quart Dutch oven, cook sausage, mushrooms, onion and garlic over medium heat until sausage is no longer pink and vegetables are tender, stirring frequently and breaking up sausage with the back of a spoon. Drain off fat. Add pasta, undrained tomatoes, tomato paste, water and red pepper flakes, stirring until combined. Transfer pasta mixture to a lightly greased 13×9×2-inch baking dish.

3. Bake, covered, at 350° for 20 minutes. Uncover and sprinkle with mozzarella cheese and Parmesan cheese. Bake, uncovered, at 350° about 10 minutes more or until heated through.

Per serving: 406 cal., 6 g total fat (2 g sat. fat), 43 mg chol., 1,276 mg sodium, 60 g carbo., 6 g fiber, 29 g pro.

Lemon Chicken Pasta Toss

When you use ingredients that contribute powerful flavors to a dish, you don't need a lot of fat to make it taste immensely satisfying. The classic Mediterranean trio of lemon, garlic and capers fills the bill in this recipe. Try it with shrimp, too.

PREP: 20 minutes
COOK: 20 minutes
MAKES: 4 servings

  2 **cups multigrain penne pasta (6 ounces)**
 12 **ounces boneless, skinless chicken breast halves, cut into 1-inch pieces**
  2 **tablespoons all-purpose flour**
  2 **tablespoons olive oil**
 ⅓ **cup finely chopped shallots**
  2 **cloves garlic, minced**
 ¾ **cup chicken broth**
  3 **tablespoons lemon juice**
 ¼ **teaspoon salt**
 ¼ **teaspoon black pepper**
  3 **tablespoons capers, drained**
  3 **tablespoons chopped Italian (flat-leaf) parsley leaves**
     Freshly grated Parmesan cheese (optional)

1. Cook pasta following package directions; drain well. Return pasta to hot saucepan; cover and keep warm.

2. While pasta is cooking, in medium-size bowl, toss together chicken and flour until chicken is lightly coated. In large skillet, cook and stir chicken in 1 tablespoon of the olive oil over medium-high heat for 6 to 8 minutes or until chicken is no longer pink. Remove chicken from pan; set aside.

3. Add remaining olive oil to skillet. Add shallots and garlic; cook and stir over medium heat about 1 minute or until tender. Carefully stir in chicken broth, lemon juice, salt and pepper. Cook, uncovered, for 2 to 3 minutes or until reduced to about ⅔ cup. Stir in chicken, capers and parsley; heat through.

4. Toss pasta with chicken mixture. If desired, sprinkle with Parmesan cheese.

Per 1½ cups: 339 cal., 9 g total fat (1 g sat. fat), 50 mg chol., 589 mg sodium, 36 g carbo., 4 g fiber, 29 g pro.

Lemon Shrimp Pasta Toss: Prepare as directed, except substitute 12 ounces peeled, deveined shrimp for chicken. Toss together shrimp and flour until shrimp is lightly coated. In large skillet, cook and stir shrimp in 1 tablespoon olive oil over medium-high heat for 2 to 3 minutes or until shrimp turn pink.

Orange Chicken Bowls

This veggie-packed one-dish dinner goes from stovetop to tabletop in less than 30 minutes.

START TO FINISH: 25 minutes
MAKES: 4 servings

- 1 teaspoon finely shredded orange peel
- ¾ cup orange juice
- 1 tablespoon cornstarch
- 3 tablespoons hoisin sauce
- 2 tablespoons cider vinegar
- ¼ cup sliced almonds
- 2 tablespoons vegetable oil
- 1 package (16 ounces) frozen pepper stir-fry vegetables (yellow, green and sweet red peppers and onion)
- 1 pound boneless, skinless chicken breast halves, cut into bite-size strips
   Salt and black pepper
- 3 cups packaged shredded cabbage with carrot (coleslaw mix)

1. In small bowl, stir together orange peel, orange juice, cornstarch, hoisin sauce and cider vinegar; set aside.

2. In large skillet, heat almonds over medium heat about 2 minutes or until lightly toasted. Remove and set aside. Add 1 tablespoon of the oil to skillet and heat over medium-high heat. Add frozen stir-fry vegetables. Cook and stir about 4 minutes or just until tender. Remove from skillet. Drain liquid and set pepper mixture aside.

3. Add remaining oil to skillet. Add chicken to skillet. Cook and stir about 3 minutes or until no longer pink. Stir orange juice mixture and add to skillet. Cook and stir until thickened and bubbly. Return vegetables to skillet; cook and stir for 1 minute. Season to taste with salt and pepper.

4. Serve chicken mixture in bowls over cabbage. Top with almonds.

Per serving: 319 cal., 12 g total fat (1 g sat. fat), 66 mg chol., 445 mg sodium, 22 g carbo., 5 g fiber, 30 g pro.

Turkey Piccata with Fettuccine

Preparing something "piccata" style simply means it's flavored with lemon, white wine, capers and parsley.

START TO FINISH: 30 minutes
MAKES: 4 servings

- 6 **ounces fettuccine or linguine**
- ¼ **cup all-purpose flour**
- ½ **teaspoon lemon-pepper seasoning or black pepper**
- 2 **turkey breast tenderloins (about 1 pound total)**
- 2 **tablespoons olive oil or vegetable oil**
- ⅓ **cup dry white wine**
- 2 **tablespoons lemon juice**
- 2 **tablespoons water**
- ½ **teaspoon instant chicken bouillon granules**
- 1 **tablespoon capers, rinsed and drained (optional)**
- 2 **tablespoons chopped fresh parsley leaves**
  Lemon wedges and fresh parsley sprigs, for garnish (optional)

1. Cook pasta following package directions. Drain well; keep warm.

2. While pasta is cooking, in small bowl, stir together flour and lemon-pepper seasoning; set aside. Cut each turkey tenderloin in half crosswise to make ½-inch pieces. Dip pieces in flour mixture to coat.

3. In large skillet, cook turkey in hot oil over medium-high heat for 6 to 10 minutes or until light golden and no longer pink, turning once halfway through cooking. Remove turkey from skillet; cover and keep warm.

4. Add wine, lemon juice, water and bouillon granules to skillet, scraping up crusty bits from bottom of skillet. If desired, stir in capers. Bring to a boil; reduce heat. Simmer, uncovered, for 2 minutes. Remove from heat; stir in chopped parsley.

5. To serve, divide pasta among 4 dinner plates. Divide turkey pieces among dinner plates. Spoon sauce over all. If desired, garnish with lemon wedges and fresh parsley sprigs.

Per serving: 391 cal., 8 g total fat (1 g sat. fat), 70 mg chol., 291 mg sodium, 39 g carbo., 2 g fiber, 34 g pro.

Mediterranean-Style Tuna Casserole

Mediterranean-Style Tuna Casserole

Here's a whole new tuna casserole. It trades the heavy, cheese-laden sauce of the classic version for a whisper-light sauce made with just a little olive oil, raisins, dried tomatoes, olives and parsley.

PREP: 25 minutes
BAKE: at 350° about 30 minutes
MAKES: 4 servings

    2 cups bow-tie pasta
    1 small onion, thinly sliced
    2 cloves garlic, minced
    1 tablespoon olive oil
    1 can (12 ounces) chunk light tuna, drained and
         broken into chunks
    ¾ cup water
    ½ cup raisins
    ½ cup dried tomatoes (not oil packed), thinly sliced
    ¼ cup oil-cured black olives, pitted and halved, or
         ¼ cup pitted kalamata olives, halved
    2 tablespoons pine nuts (optional)
    1 tablespoon chopped fresh parsley leaves
    ½ cup finely shredded Parmesan cheese (2 ounces)
    ½ cup coarsely torn fresh basil leaves

1. Heat oven to 350°. Cook pasta following package directions. Drain well.

2. While pasta is cooking, in large ovenproof skillet, cook onion and garlic in hot olive oil over medium heat until onion is tender, stirring occasionally. Add tuna, water, raisins, tomatoes, olives, pine nuts, if desired, and parsley to onion mixture. Stir in cooked pasta.

3. Bake in skillet, covered, at 350° for 25 minutes. Uncover and sprinkle with cheese. Bake, uncovered, at 350° about 5 minutes more or until heated through and cheese is melted. Sprinkle with basil before serving.

Per serving: 332 cal., 8 g total fat (3 g sat. fat), 33 mg chol., 678 mg sodium, 35 g carbo., 3 g fiber, 30 g pro.

Almond-Herbed Salmon

A flavorful and satisfying crust of fresh bread crumbs, almonds and herbs gives this baked salmon loads of flavor without the addition of butter or other fats.

PREP: 20 minutes
BAKE: at 400° for 10 to 12 minutes
MAKES: 4 servings

   Nonstick cooking spray
 1 slice whole wheat bread, torn
 ¼ cup sliced almonds
 2 tablespoons chopped fresh basil leaves
 2 tablespoons chopped shallots
 1 tablespoon chopped fresh parsley leaves
 ½ teaspoon salt
 1 clove garlic, minced
 4 salmon fillets (5 ounces each, 1 inch thick)
 2 tablespoons lemon juice
 ¼ teaspoon black pepper
   Lemon wedges and/or fresh basil leaves, for
   garnish (optional)

1. Heat oven to 400°. Lightly coat shallow baking pan with nonstick cooking spray; set pan aside. In food processor or blender, combine bread, almonds, 2 tablespoons basil, shallots, parsley, ¼ teaspoon of the salt and garlic. Cover and process or blend until coarsely chopped.

2. Thaw salmon, if frozen. Rinse salmon; pat dry with paper towels. Place salmon in prepared baking pan; drizzle with lemon juice. Sprinkle with the remaining ¼ teaspoon salt and the pepper. Gently pat some of the bread crumb mixture on top of each salmon fillet.

3. Bake, uncovered, at 400° for 10 to 12 minutes or until fish flakes when tested with a fork. If desired, garnish with lemon wedges and/or additional basil.

Per serving: 221 cal., 8 g total fat (1 g sat. fat), 74 mg chol., 420 mg sodium, 6 g carbo., 1 g fiber, 30 g pro.

Almond-Herbed Salmon

Orange-Rosemary Tuna

This tapas-style dish—served chilled—is lovely as part of an appetizer-buffet-as-dinner on a warm summer night. Serve it with a chilled (of course) dry white wine. It makes a just-right entrée for four people, as well.

PREP: 20 minutes
GRILL: 6 minutes
CHILL: 1 hour
MAKES: 8 servings

- 2 **fresh or frozen tuna steaks (8 ounces each, cut 1 inch thick)**
- 1 **tablespoon olive oil**
- 1 **tablespoon orange juice**
- ⅓ **cup mayonnaise**
- ¼ **cup finely chopped red onion**
- 1 **teaspoon finely shredded orange peel**
- ½ **of a medium-size orange, peeled, seeded, sectioned and coarsely chopped**
- 1 **teaspoon chopped fresh rosemary**
- ¼ **teaspoon freshly ground black pepper**
  Orange peel strips and chopped fresh rosemary, for garnish (optional)
  Small Armenian cracker bread (lahvosh) or black pepper crackers, for serving (optional)

1. Thaw tuna, if frozen. Rinse fish; pat dry with paper towels. In small bowl, combine olive oil and orange juice. Brush tuna with oil mixture.

2. Grease grill rack. Heat gas grill to medium or prepare charcoal grill with medium coals. Grill fish for 4 to 6 minutes or until tuna is slightly pink in center. Turn tuna over once, halfway through grilling. Remove tuna from grill. Cover and refrigerate tuna about 1 hour or until completely chilled. Slice to serve.

3. In small bowl, combine mayonnaise, onion, 1 teaspoon orange peel, chopped orange, 1 teaspoon rosemary and pepper. Divide tuna among 8 plates. Top each serving with 1 tablespoon of the mayonnaise mixture. If desired, in small bowl, combine orange peel strips and additional rosemary; sprinkle over tuna. If desired, serve with crackers.

Per serving: 147 cal., 9 g total fat (2 g sat. fat), 29 mg chol., 71 mg sodium, 1 g carbo., 0 g fiber, 13 g pro.

Tortilla-Black Bean Casserole

Layered a bit like lasagna, this hearty but healthy casserole is decidedly Mexican. Corn tortillas, well-seasoned black beans and reduced-fat cheese are baked until bubbly, then topped with cool and crisp lettuce, tomato, scallions and olives.

PREP: 25 minutes
BAKE: at 350° for 30 to 35 minutes
STAND: 10 minutes
MAKES: 8 servings

- 2 **large onions, chopped (2 cups)**
- 2 **medium-size green peppers, chopped (1½ cups)**
- 1 **can (15 ounces) tomatoes, cut up**
- ¾ **cup picante sauce or green salsa**
- 2 **teaspoons ground cumin**
- 2 **cloves garlic, minced**
- 2 **cans (15 ounces each) black beans and/or red kidney beans, rinsed and drained**
- 12 **(6-inch) corn tortillas**
- 2 **cups shredded reduced-fat Monterey Jack cheese (8 ounces)**
  Chopped fresh tomatoes, shredded lettuce, sliced scallions and sliced pitted ripe olives, for serving (optional)
- ½ **cup light sour cream or plain low-fat yogurt, for serving (optional)**

1. Heat oven to 350°. In large skillet, combine onions, green peppers, undrained tomatoes, picante sauce, cumin and garlic. Bring to a boil; reduce heat. Simmer, uncovered, for 10 minutes. Stir in beans.

2. Spread one-third of the bean mixture over the bottom of 13×9×2-inch baking dish. Top with 6 of the tortillas, overlapping as necessary, and 1 cup of the cheese. Add another one-third of the bean mixture; top with remaining tortillas and remaining bean mixture.

3. Bake, covered, at 350° for 30 to 35 minutes or until heated through. Sprinkle with remaining cheese. Let stand for 10 minutes before serving.

4. If desired, top with chopped tomato, lettuce, scallions and olives. If desired, serve with sour cream.

Per serving: 273 cal., 8 g total fat (4 g sat. fat), 20 mg chol., 772 mg sodium, 42 g carbo., 9 g fiber, 17 g pro.

Chapter 7

Bring A Dish

Sharing a meal—especially the making of it—with friends and family is satisfying and sociable. Pick a dish from these potluck-perfect recipes for your next gathering, and it's sure to be a hit.

Jumbo Shell Pasta Stuffed
with Baby White Cheddar
and Chicken Macaroni

Jumbo Shell Pasta Stuffed with Baby White Cheddar and Chicken Macaroni

Right before the entry deadline for the 2007 Tillamook® Macaroni & Cheese Recipe Contest, Lorie Roach stood in her San Antonio, Texas, supermarket, surveying the different kinds of pasta. "I saw the big shells right next to the little shells, and I thought it would be great to stuff them inside," she says. The judges thought so, too. She nabbed the $5,000 grand prize.

PREP: 1 hour
BAKE: at 400° about 20 minutes
MAKES: 8 to 10 main-dish servings

- 6 ounces small shell macaroni (2 cups)
- 12 ounces jumbo shell macaroni (40)
- ¼ cup (½ stick) Tillamook® salted butter
- ¼ cup all-purpose flour
- 2 cups whole milk
- 1 cup half-and-half or light cream
- 1 teaspoon salt
- 1 teaspoon cracked black pepper
- 3 cups shredded Tillamook® Vintage White Extra-Sharp Cheddar Cheese (12 ounces)
- 2 cups shredded cooked chicken
- ¾ cup chopped oil-packed dried tomatoes, well drained
   Nonstick cooking spray
- 1 cup finely crushed cornflakes
- 2 tablespoons (¼ stick) Tillamook® salted butter, melted

1. Heat oven to 400°. Cook small and jumbo shell macaroni separately following package directions. Drain well; set aside.

2. In heavy, large saucepan, melt the ¼ cup butter over medium heat; add flour and whisk for 1 minute. Gradually whisk in milk and half-and-half; cook over medium-high heat, stirring constantly, until thickened and bubbly. Stir in salt and pepper. Gradually add 2 cups of the shredded cheese, stirring until melted. Stir in the small shell macaroni, chicken and dried tomatoes. Cool slightly, about 10 minutes.

3. Coat 13×9×2-inch baking dish with nonstick cooking spray. Carefully fill each jumbo shell with the chicken mixture; arrange filled shells in baking dish. Spoon any remaining chicken mixture over filled shells. Sprinkle with remaining 1 cup cheese. Stir together cornflakes and the 2 tablespoons melted butter. Sprinkle evenly over the tops of the shells.

4. Bake, uncovered, at 400° about 20 minutes or until golden brown and bubbly.

Per serving: 676 cal., 33 g total fat (19 g sat. fat), 116 mg chol., 748 mg sodium, 61 g carbo., 3 g fiber, 33 g pro.

Deb's Hot Rod Chili

When Debbie Ashman entered the 2007 Terlingua International Chili Championship—the granddaddy of all chili cook-offs—she was hardly a seasoned hand on the chili circuit. She and her husband had moved to Bastrop, Texas, from Alaska just two years before. But it was her hand with seasonings that won her the grand prize. "I was stunned," she says.

PREP: 20 minutes
COOK: 2 hours
MAKES: 6 main-dish servings

- 2 **pounds coarsely ground beef**
- 1 **can (8 ounces) El Pato® tomato sauce**
- 1 **can (14 ounces) beef broth**
- 1¾ **cups water**
- **Spice Mix 1 (see recipe, right)**
- **Spice Mix 2 (see recipe, right)**
- **Spice Mix 3 (see recipe, right)**
- **Cornbread, for serving (optional)**

1. In 6-quart Dutch oven, cook beef over medium heat until browned; drain off fat. Stir in tomato sauce, broth and the water. Bring to a boil. Stir in Spice Mix 1. Reduce heat; cover and simmer for 1 hour.

2. Add Spice Mix 2. Cover and simmer for 45 minutes more.

3. Add Spice Mix 3; simmer, uncovered, for 15 minutes.

4. If desired, serve with cornbread.

Spice Mix 1: In small bowl, combine 1 tablespoon onion powder, 2 teaspoons garlic powder, 2 teaspoons instant beef bouillon granules, 1 teaspoon instant chicken bouillon granules, 1 tablespoon Pacifica Beauty Paprika*, 1 tablespoon Mexene® Chili Powder*, ½ teaspoon cayenne pepper, ¼ teaspoon black pepper and 1 package Sazon Goya®*. Makes about ¼ cup.

Spice Mix 2: In small bowl, combine 1 tablespoon Mexene® Chili Powder*, 1 tablespoon Hatch Mild Chili Powder*, 2 tablespoons Cowtown Light Chili Powder*, 1 teaspoon ground cumin and ¼ teaspoon ground white pepper. Makes about ¼ cup.

Spice Mix 3: In small bowl, combine 1 teaspoon onion powder, 1 teaspoon garlic salt, ¼ teaspoon cayenne pepper, ¾ tablespoon Cowtown Light Chili Powder* and 1 tablespoon ground cumin. Makes about 2 tablespoons.

*Note: These spices are available online from Mild Bill's Spices at www.mildbills.com

Per serving: 387 cal., 24 g total fat (9 g sat. fat), 103 mg chol., 1,318 mg sodium, 10 g carbo., 4 g fiber, 31 g pro.

Deb's Hot Rod Chili

Savory Bean Salad

Colorful and fresh, here's a slightly different kind of bean salad to bring to a summer party.

PREP: 25 minutes
CHILL: 2 to 8 hours
MAKES: 12 side-dish servings

- 1 can (15 ounces) garbanzo beans (chickpeas), rinsed and drained
- ½ of a can (15 ounces) black beans, rinsed and drained (1 cup)
- 2 jars (6 ounces each) marinated artichoke hearts, drained and coarsely chopped (1½ cups)
- 2 medium-size tomatoes, chopped (2 cups)
- ½ cup crumbled feta cheese (2 ounces)
- ¼ cup finely chopped Vidalia or red onion
- ¼ cup chopped fresh cilantro leaves
- ¼ cup olive oil
- 2 tablespoons lemon juice
- 3 cloves garlic, minced
  Sliced baguette-style French bread, toasted (optional)

1. In large bowl, combine garbanzo beans, black beans, artichoke hearts, tomatoes, feta cheese, onion and fresh cilantro.

2. In small bowl, whisk together olive oil, lemon juice and garlic. Pour over bean mixture; toss gently to coat. Cover and refrigerate for at least 2 hours or up to 8 hours. If desired, serve with toasted baguette slices.

Per serving: 126 cal., 8 g total fat (2 g sat. fat), 6 mg chol., 325 mg sodium, 12 g carbo., 2 g fiber, 4 g pro.

Vegetable Pasta Salad

Everybody loves pasta salad, and this one goes with just about anything you can cook on a grill. Lots of fresh vegetables, herbs and balsamic vinaigrette make it especially appealing.

PREP: 25 minutes
CHILL: 4 to 24 hours
MAKES: 16 side-dish servings

- 2 cups mostaccioli or penne pasta
- 6 ounces provolone cheese, cut into ¾-inch cubes
- 1 small zucchini, halved lengthwise and thinly sliced (1 cup)
- 1 cup halved cherry tomatoes
- 1 small red onion, thinly sliced and separated into rings
- ¾ cup chopped sweet red or green pepper
- 1 can (2¼ ounces) sliced pitted ripe olives, drained
- 2 ounces Parmesan cheese, shaved
- ¼ cup chopped fresh parsley leaves
- ¾ cup bottled balsamic vinaigrette salad dressing

1. Cook pasta following package directions; drain well. Rinse with cold water; drain again.

2. In very large bowl, combine pasta, provolone cheese, zucchini, cherry tomatoes, onion, pepper, olives, Parmesan cheese and parsley. Add dressing; toss to coat. Cover and refrigerate for at least 4 hours or up to 24 hours.

Per serving: 132 cal., 8 g total fat (3 g sat. fat), 10 mg chol., 326 mg sodium, 10 g carbo., 1 g fiber, 6 g pro.

24-Hour Vegetable Salad

This fix-and-forget potluck classic is best made in a clear glass bowl or dish so you can see the pretty layers. Since the early 1980s, when it first became popular, it has been a surefire favorite with super-busy cooks.

PREP: 30 minutes
CHILL: 2 to 24 hours
MAKES: 6 to 8 side-dish servings

4	cups torn iceberg lettuce, romaine lettuce, leaf lettuce, Bibb lettuce and/or fresh spinach Salt and black pepper (optional)
1	cup sliced fresh mushrooms, broccoli florets or frozen peas
1	cup shredded carrots (2 medium-size)
2	hard-cooked eggs, sliced
6	strips bacon, crisp-cooked, drained and crumbled
¾	cup shredded American, Cheddar or Swiss cheese (3 ounces)
¼	cup thinly sliced scallions (2)
¾	cup mayonnaise
1	tablespoon lemon juice
1½	teaspoons chopped fresh dill or ½ teaspoon dried dill Thinly sliced scallions (optional)

1. Place lettuce in 2- or 2½-quart salad bowl. If desired, sprinkle with salt and pepper. Layer on top of lettuce in the following order: mushrooms; carrots; eggs; bacon; ½ cup of the cheese and the ¼ cup scallions.

2. In small bowl, combine mayonnaise, lemon juice and dill. Spread mayonnaise mixture over top of salad. Sprinkle with remaining ¼ cup cheese. If desired, garnish with additional scallions. Cover salad tightly with plastic wrap. Refrigerate for at least 2 hours or up to 24 hours. To serve, toss to coat vegetables.

Per serving: 342 cal., 32 g total fat (8 g sat. fat), 103 mg chol., 586 mg sodium, 5 g carbo., 1 g fiber, 9 g pro.

Crunchy Oriental Cabbage Slaw

This light and crunchy vinaigrette-dressed slaw is a great alternative to heavier mayonnaise-based slaws that may not be the best choice for an outdoor picnic on a warm day.

START TO FINISH: 15 minutes
MAKES: 8 to 10 side-dish servings

- ⅓ **cup vegetable oil**
- ⅓ **cup rice vinegar or vinegar**
- 2 **tablespoons sugar**
- 2 **teaspoons soy sauce**
- ¼ **teaspoon black pepper or ⅛ teaspoon red pepper flakes**
- 1 **package (3 ounces) chicken- or beef-flavored ramen noodles, broken**
- ½ **of a package (16 ounces) shredded cabbage with carrot (coleslaw mix, about 4 cups) or 3 cups shredded green cabbage and 1 cup shredded red cabbage**
- ½ **cup slivered almonds, toasted**
- ¼ **cup sliced scallions (2)**
- ¼ **cup shelled sunflower seeds or 2 tablespoons sesame seeds**

1. In small bowl, whisk together oil, vinegar, sugar, soy sauce, black pepper and the contents of seasoning packet from ramen noodles. Set dressing aside.

2. In large bowl, combine the broken dry ramen noodles, cabbage, almonds, scallions and sunflower seeds. Drizzle oil mixture over the cabbage mixture. Toss to coat. Serve immediately or cover and refrigerate up to 1 hour before serving.

Per serving: 201 cal., 16 g total fat (2 g sat. fat), 0 mg chol., 200 mg sodium, 11 g carbo., 2 g fiber, 4 g pro.

Apple-Rice Salad

This autumnal salad makes a great accompaniment to roast pork or pork chops. Serve it on plates lined with tender and pretty leaves of butterhead or Boston lettuce.

PREP: 50 minutes
CHILL: 2 to 6 hours
MAKES: 6 side-dish servings

- ⅓ cup uncooked brown rice
- ⅓ cup uncooked wild rice, rinsed and drained
- 1¾ cups water
- 2 medium-size apples, chopped (2 cups)
- 2 ribs celery, thinly sliced (1 cup)
- ¼ cup shelled sunflower seeds
- ¼ cup dried currants or dried cranberries
- 2 tablespoons balsamic vinegar
- 1 tablespoon olive oil
- 2 teaspoons honey
- 2 teaspoons brown or Dijon mustard
- 2 teaspoons finely shredded orange peel
- 1 clove garlic, minced
- ¼ teaspoon salt
- Lettuce leaves (optional)

1. In medium-size saucepan, combine brown rice and wild rice. Add the water. Bring to a boil; reduce heat. Cover and simmer for 40 to 45 minutes or until rice is tender. Drain. Transfer rice mixture to large bowl; cover and refrigerate for 2 hours.

2. Add apple, celery, sunflower seeds and currants to chilled rice mixture; stir to combine. In screw-top jar, combine vinegar, olive oil, honey, mustard, orange peel, garlic and salt. Cover and shake well. Pour over rice mixture; toss gently to coat. Serve immediately or cover and refrigerate for up to 4 hours. If desired, serve on lettuce-lined plates.

Per serving: 184 cal., 6 g total fat (1 g sat. fat), 0 mg chol., 134 mg sodium, 31 g carbo., 3 g fiber, 4 g pro.

Baked Bean Quintet

Bring this saucy five-bean side to your next potluck, and yours will be the best baked beans on the buffet table.

PREP: 25 minutes
BAKE: at 375° about 1 hour
MAKES: 12 to 16 side-dish servings

- 6 strips bacon, chopped
- 1 cup chopped onion (1 large)
- 1 clove garlic, minced
- 1 can (21 ounces) pork and beans in tomato sauce
- 1 can (15 to 16 ounces) butter or lima beans, drained
- 1 can (15 to 16 ounces) red kidney beans, rinsed and drained
- 1 can (15 to 19 ounces) cannellini (white kidney) beans, rinsed and drained
- 1 can (15 ounces) garbanzo beans (chickpeas), rinsed and drained
- ¾ cup ketchup
- ½ cup molasses
- ¼ cup packed brown sugar
- 1 tablespoon yellow mustard
- 1 tablespoon Worcestershire sauce

1. Heat oven to 375°. In large skillet, cook bacon, onion and garlic over medium heat until bacon is crisp and onion is tender; drain well. In ungreased 3-quart casserole, combine onion mixture, undrained pork and beans, the butter beans, kidney beans, cannellini beans, garbanzo beans, ketchup, molasses, brown sugar, mustard and Worcestershire sauce. Mix well.

2. Bake, covered, at 375° about 1 hour or until bubbly and heated through.

Per serving: 246 cal., 5 g total fat (2 g sat. fat), 9 mg chol., 842 mg sodium, 50 g carbo., 5 g fiber, 12 g pro.

Creamy Potluck Potatoes

These yummy potatoes go with so many things, they're a good fit for whatever the main dish is—whether it's ham, burgers on the grill, baked chicken or something else.

PREP: 25 minutes
BAKE: at 350° for 25 to 30 minutes
STAND: 5 minutes
MAKES: 10 side-dish servings

- 3 pounds potatoes, peeled and cut up (about 6 cups)
- 1 can (10¾ ounces) reduced-sodium condensed cream of chicken soup
- ½ cup sour cream
- 1 package (3 ounces) cream cheese, softened
- 2 tablespoons butter, melted
- ¾ cup shredded Cheddar cheese (3 ounces)
- ¼ cup sliced scallions (2)
- ¼ cup milk
- ¼ teaspoon garlic salt
- ¼ teaspoon black pepper

1. Heat oven to 350°. In large saucepan, cook potatoes, covered, in enough boiling, salted water to cover for 10 to 12 minutes or just until tender. Drain; rinse with cold water. Drain again.

2. While potatoes are cooking, in large bowl, stir together soup, sour cream, cream cheese and butter. Stir in ¼ cup of the Cheddar cheese, 3 tablespoons of the scallions, the milk, garlic salt and pepper. Stir in the cooked potatoes. Transfer potato mixture to 12×8×2-inch baking dish.

3. Bake at 350° for 25 to 30 minutes or until heated through. Sprinkle with the remaining ½ cup Cheddar cheese. Let stand about 5 minutes or until cheese melts. Sprinkle with the remaining 1 tablespoon scallion.

Per serving: 237 cal., 11 g total fat (7 g sat. fat), 32 mg chol., 275 mg sodium, 29 g carbo., 2 g fiber, 7 g pro.

Creamed Corn Casserole

The slow cooker version of this dish (see variation, below) is perfect for those middle-of-the-week gatherings—such as book club or a church meeting—when you need to bring a side dish to share. Assemble it before you leave the house, and it's ready when you come home.

PREP: 15 minutes
BAKE: at 375° for 50 to 55 minutes
MAKES: 12 side-dish servings

Nonstick cooking spray
2 packages (16 ounces each) frozen whole kernel corn
2 cups chopped sweet red and/or green pepper (2 large)
1 cup chopped onion (1 large)
1 tablespoon butter
¼ teaspoon black pepper
1 can (10¾ ounces) condensed cream of celery soup
1 tub (8 ounces) cream cheese spread with chive and onion or cream cheese spread with garden vegetables
¼ cup milk

1. Heat oven to 375°. Lightly coat 2-quart casserole with nonstick cooking spray; set aside. Place corn in a colander and thaw by running under cold water; drain. Set aside.

2. In large saucepan, cook red and/or green pepper and onion in 1 tablespoon hot butter until tender. Stir in corn and black pepper. In medium-size bowl, whisk together soup, cream cheese spread and milk. Stir soup mixture into corn mixture. Transfer to prepared casserole.

3. Bake, covered, at 375° for 50 to 55 minutes or until heated through, stirring once.

Per serving: 176 cal., 9 g total fat (5 g sat. fat), 22 mg chol., 280 mg sodium, 22 g carbo., 3 g fiber, 4 g pro.

Slow cooker directions: Do not thaw corn and omit butter. In 3½- or 4-quart slow cooker, combine frozen corn, red and/or green peppers, onion and black pepper. In medium-size bowl, whisk together soup, cream cheese and milk. Pour over mixture in cooker. Cover and cook on low-heat setting for 8 to 10 hours or on high-heat setting for 4 to 5 hours. Stir before serving.

Checkerboard Rolls

Frozen rolls get dressed up with flavorful toppings and the result is as pretty to look at as they are good to eat.

PREP: 20 minutes
CHILL: 8 to 24 hours
STAND: 45 minutes
BAKE: at 375° for 20 to 25 minutes
MAKES: 16 rolls

- 2 **tablespoons poppy seeds**
- 2 **tablespoons sesame seeds**
- 1 **teaspoon lemon-pepper seasoning**
- 2 **tablespoons yellow cornmeal**
- 2 **tablespoons grated or finely shredded Parmesan cheese**
- 3 **tablespoons butter, melted**
- 16 **pieces (1.3 ounces each) frozen white roll dough**

1. Grease 9×9×2-inch square pan; set aside. In shallow dish, combine poppy seeds, sesame seeds and lemon-pepper seasoning. In another shallow dish, combine cornmeal and Parmesan cheese. Place butter in third dish. Working quickly, roll dough pieces in butter, then in one of the seasoning mixtures to lightly coat. (Coat half of the rolls with one seasoning mixture and the remaining rolls with the other seasoning mixture.) Alternate rolls in prepared pan. Cover rolls with greased plastic wrap. Let thaw in refrigerator for at least 8 hours or up to 24 hours.

2. Remove pan from refrigerator; uncover and let stand at room temperature for 45 minutes. After 35 minutes, heat oven to 375°.

3. Bake rolls at 375° for 20 to 25 minutes or until golden. Remove rolls from pan to wire rack. Cool slightly. Serve warm.

Per roll: 136 cal., 5 g total fat (2 g sat. fat), 6 mg chol., 189 mg sodium, 19 g carbo., 1 g fiber, 4 g pro.

Garlic-Herb Checkerboard Rolls: Prepare as above, except in Step 1 omit lemon-pepper seasoning. Add 1 teaspoon dried Italian seasoning and ½ teaspoon garlic powder to the seed mixture.

Tex-Mex Chicken 'n' Rice Casserole

Twice the rice is always nice. This tasty dish contains both a rice and vermicelli mix and long-grain rice. It gets its great Tex-Mex style and flavor from chiles, chili powder and cumin.

PREP: 25 minutes
BAKE: at 425° for 25 minutes
STAND: 5 minutes
MAKES: 12 main-dish servings

- 1 **large onion, chopped (1 cup)**
- 2 **tablespoons olive oil**
- 1 **package (6.9 ounces) chicken-flavored rice and vermicelli mix**
- 1 **cup uncooked long-grain rice**
- 2 **cans (14 ounces each) chicken broth**
- 2½ **cups water**
- 4 **cups chopped cooked chicken**
- 4 **medium-size tomatoes, chopped (2 cups)**
- 1 **can (4 ounces) diced green chiles, drained**
- 1 **tablespoon chili powder**
- 2 **teaspoons dried basil**
- ¼ **teaspoon ground cumin**
- ¼ **teaspoon black pepper**
- 1 **cup shredded Cheddar cheese (4 ounces)**

1. Heat oven to 425°. In 3-quart saucepan, cook onion in hot olive oil until tender. Stir in rice and vermicelli mix (including seasoning package) and uncooked long-grain rice. Cook and stir for 2 minutes. Stir in chicken broth and water. Bring to a boil; reduce heat. Cover and simmer for 20 minutes (liquid will not be fully absorbed).

2. Transfer rice mixture to very large bowl. Stir in chicken, tomatoes, chiles, chili powder, basil, cumin and black pepper. Transfer to 3-quart casserole.

3. Bake, covered, at 425° for 25 minutes. Uncover and sprinkle with Cheddar cheese. Let stand for 5 minutes before serving.

Make-ahead directions: Prepare casserole; cover and refrigerate for up to 24 hours. Heat oven to 425°. Bake, covered, at 425° about 40 minutes or until heated through. Uncover and sprinkle with cheese. Let stand for 5 minutes before serving.

Per serving: 281 cal., 10 g total fat (3 g sat. fat), 52 mg chol., 659 mg sodium, 28 g carbo., 2 g fiber, 19 g pro.

Potluck Chicken Tetrazzini

Potluck Chicken Tetrazzini

You know a dish is good when it stands the test of time. This one was created more than a century ago—probably between 1908 and 1910—in honor of Italian-born opera star Luisa Tetrazzini.

PREP: 30 minutes
BAKE: at 350° about 15 minutes
STAND: 5 minutes
MAKES: 10 main-dish servings

- 1 purchased rotisserie chicken
- 8 ounces spaghetti or linguine, broken in half
- ¾ pound fresh asparagus, trimmed and cut into 1-inch pieces
- ½ pound small whole fresh mushrooms*
- 3 medium-size sweet red and/or yellow peppers, seeded and cut into 1-inch pieces
- 2 tablespoons butter
- ¼ cup all-purpose flour
- ⅛ teaspoon black pepper
- 1 can (14 ounces) chicken broth
- ¾ cup milk
- ½ cup shredded Swiss cheese (2 ounces)
- 1 tablespoon finely shredded lemon peel
- 2 slices sourdough bread, cut into cubes (about 1½ cups)
- 1 tablespoon olive oil
- 2 tablespoons chopped fresh parsley leaves

1. Heat oven to 350°. Remove meat from chicken; discard bones. Cut chicken pieces in chunks to equal 3 cups. Save remaining chicken for another use.

2. In Dutch oven, cook pasta following package directions. Add asparagus the last 1 minute of cooking. Drain well. Return pasta and asparagus to Dutch oven.

3. While pasta is cooking, in large skillet, cook mushrooms and sweet peppers in hot butter over medium heat for 8 to 10 minutes or until mushrooms are tender, stirring occasionally. Stir in flour and black pepper. Add chicken broth and milk all at once. Cook and stir until thickened and bubbly.

4. Add mushroom mixture, chicken, Swiss cheese and half the lemon peel to pasta mixture in Dutch oven. Toss gently to coat. Spoon pasta mixture into 13×9×2-inch baking dish.

5. In medium-size bowl, toss together bread cubes, olive oil and remaining lemon peel. Sprinkle bread cube mixture over pasta mixture.

6. Bake, uncovered, at 350° about 15 minutes or until heated through. Let stand for 5 minutes before serving. Sprinkle with parsley before serving.

*Note: If mushrooms are large, cut them in halves or quarters so they are all about 1- to 1½-inch pieces.

To transport: Do not let mixture stand after baking. Cover with heavy-duty foil. Wrap dish in several layers of newspaper or a heavy towel. Then place in an insulated container. Serve within 2 hours. Transport parsley in separate container or plastic bag.

Per serving: 282 cal., 10 g total fat (4 g sat. fat), 48 mg chol., 258 mg sodium, 28 g carbo., 2 g fiber, 20 g pro.

Italian Crescent Casserole

Any kind of tomato-based pasta sauce works well in this dish—marinara, spicy, sausage, four-cheese, olive, chunky vegetable—whatever you like best.

PREP: 25 minutes
BAKE: at 375° for 20 to 25 minutes
MAKES: 12 main-dish servings

    2   pounds lean ground beef
    1   medium-size onion, chopped (½ cup)
    2   cups tomato pasta sauce
    3   cups shredded mozzarella or Monterey Jack
        cheese (12 ounces)
    1   carton (8 ounces) sour cream
    1   tube (8 ounces) refrigerated crescent rolls (8)
    2   tablespoons (¼ stick) butter, melted
    ½   cup grated Parmesan cheese

1. Heat oven to 375°. In 12-inch skillet, cook ground beef and onion until meat is brown and onion is tender; drain off fat. Stir in pasta sauce; heat through. Spread meat mixture in an ungreased 13×9×2-inch baking dish.

2. Combine mozzarella cheese and sour cream; spoon over meat mixture in baking dish.

3. Unroll crescent rolls, but do not separate into triangles. On a lightly floured surface, press dough edges together and roll out slightly to fit dish. Place dough over the cheese layer. Brush with melted butter and sprinkle with Parmesan cheese.

4. Bake, uncovered, at 375° for 20 to 25 minutes or until top is deep golden brown.

Per serving: 405 cal., 29 g total fat (13 g sat. fat), 83 mg chol., 675 mg sodium, 14 g carbo., 1 g fiber, 25 g pro.

Mexican Mac and Beef Casserole

Lighten up this kid-pleasing casserole a bit by using ground beef that is 90-93 percent lean, light sour cream and reduced-fat cheese.

PREP: 20 minutes
BAKE: at 350° about 30 minutes
MAKES: 8 main-dish servings

    2   cups elbow macaroni (8 ounces)
    1½ pounds lean ground beef
    2½ cups picante sauce or salsa
    1   can (15 ounces) black beans, rinsed and drained
    2   teaspoons dried oregano
    1   teaspoon ground cumin
    1   teaspoon chili powder
    ¾   teaspoon garlic powder
    1   carton (16 ounces) sour cream
    ¾   cup sliced scallions (6)
    1   can (2¼ ounces drained weight) sliced ripe olives,
        drained
    1   cup shredded Monterey Jack cheese (4 ounces)

1. Preheat oven to 350°. In 4- to 5-quart Dutch oven, cook macaroni following package directions; drain well. Return macaroni to Dutch oven; set aside.

2. While macaroni is cooking, in large skillet, cook ground beef over medium heat until brown; drain off fat.

3. Stir cooked beef into macaroni in Dutch oven. Stir in picante sauce, beans, oregano, cumin, chili powder and garlic powder. Transfer mixture to 3-quart casserole.

4. Bake, covered, at 350° about 25 minutes or until heated through. In medium-size bowl, stir together sour cream, scallions and olives. Spread sour cream mixture over top of casserole. Sprinkle with cheese. Bake, uncovered, at 350° about 5 minutes more or until cheese melts.

Per serving: 500 cal., 27 g total fat (14 g sat. fat), 93 mg chol., 744 mg sodium, 36 g carbo., 5 g fiber, 31 g pro.

Chili Corn Bread Pie

Refrigerated corn bread twists make a quick and easy crust for this Tex-Mex-style pie.

PREP: 35 minutes
BAKE: at 375° for 30 minutes
STAND: 10 minutes
MAKES: 8 main-dish servings

- ¾ pound lean ground beef
- 1 medium-size onion, chopped (½ cup)
- ½ cup coarsely chopped green pepper
- 1 can (15 ounces) chili beans with chili gravy or chili beans
- 1 can (8 ounces) tomato sauce
- 1 can (6 ounces) tomato paste
- 2 to 3 tablespoons chili powder
- ½ teaspoon ground cumin
- ½ teaspoon hot-pepper sauce
- 1 tube (11½ ounces) refrigerated corn bread twists (8)
- 1 carton (8 ounces) sour cream
- 2 tablespoons all-purpose flour
- 1 cup shredded Cheddar cheese (4 ounces)
- 2 cups corn chips, coarsely crushed (about 1 cup)
  Chopped green pepper (optional)

1. Heat oven to 375°. In large skillet, cook ground beef, onion and ½ cup green pepper until ground beef is brown; drain off fat. Stir in undrained beans, tomato sauce, tomato paste, chili powder, cumin and hot-pepper sauce. Bring to a boil; reduce heat. Simmer, uncovered, for 5 minutes, stirring frequently.

2. Lightly grease 9- or 10-inch pie plate. Unwrap and separate corn bread twists, but do not uncoil. Arrange corn bread coils in pie plate, pressing onto the bottom and up the sides, extending about ½ inch above edge of pie plate.

3. Spoon ground beef mixture into corn bread crust. Stir together sour cream and flour; spread evenly over ground beef mixture. Sprinkle with cheese and crushed chips. Place on a baking sheet.

4. Bake, uncovered, at 375° for 30 minutes. Let stand for 10 minutes before serving. If desired, garnish with additional chopped green pepper.

Per serving: 478 cal., 27 g total fat (12 g sat. fat), 62 mg chol., 921 mg sodium, 38 g carbo., 4 g fiber, 21 g pro.

Cheeseburger and Fries Casserole

Kids will gobble up this clever casserole-style take on one of their favorite meals.

PREP: 15 minutes
BAKE: at 350° for 45 to 55 minutes
MAKES: 8 to 10 main-dish servings

- 2 pounds lean ground beef
- 1 can (10¾ ounces) condensed golden mushroom soup
- 1 can (10¾ ounces) condensed Cheddar cheese soup
- 1 package (20 ounces) frozen fried crinkle-cut potatoes
  Ketchup, pickles, mustard and chopped tomato, for serving (optional)

1. Heat oven to 350°. In large skillet, cook ground beef, half at a time, over medium heat until brown. Drain off fat. Spread cooked beef over bottom of a 13×9×2-inch baking dish.

2. In medium-size bowl, stir together mushroom and cheese soups. Spread soup mixture over beef. Sprinkle the potatoes over the soup layer.

3. Bake, uncovered, at 350° for 45 to 55 minutes or until the potatoes are golden. If desired, serve with ketchup, pickles, mustard and tomato.

Per serving: 410 cal., 24 g total fat (8 g sat. fat), 82 mg chol., 656 mg sodium, 24 g carbo., 2 g fiber, 24 g pro.

Chicken Chow Mein Casserole

The combination of creamy filling and a crunchy chow mein topping makes this potluck perennial irresistible.

PREP: 25 minutes
BAKE: at 350° for 50 to 55 minutes
MAKES: 8 main-dish servings

- 4 cups chopped cooked chicken
- 2 cups chopped celery (4 ribs)
- 1 cup shredded carrots (2 medium-size)
- 1 cup chopped green pepper (1 large)
- 2 cans (4 ounces each) sliced mushrooms, drained
- ⅔ cup sliced or slivered almonds, toasted
- 2 tablespoons diced pimiento, drained
- 2 cans (10¾ ounces each) condensed cream of chicken soup
- 2 cups chow mein noodles

1. Heat oven to 350°. In very large bowl, stir together chicken, celery, carrots, green pepper, mushrooms, almonds and pimiento. Add soup to chicken mixture; mix well. Transfer chicken mixture to 13×9×2-inch baking dish.

2. Bake, covered, at 350° for 45 minutes. Uncover and top with chow mein noodles. Bake, uncovered, for 5 to 10 minutes more or until heated through.

Per serving: 354 cal., 19 g total fat (4 g sat. fat), 68 mg chol., 922 mg sodium, 20 g carbo., 3 g fiber, 26 g pro.

Cajun Chicken Pasta

This rich and creamy dish is ideal for time-pressed cooks. It can be assembled up to 24 hours before baking, so you can arrive at the party—hot dish in hand—cool as a cucumber.

PREP: 50 minutes
BAKE: at 350° for 25 to 30 minutes
MAKES: 8 to 10 main-dish servings

- 1 **pound bow tie or rotini pasta**
- 4 **boneless, skinless chicken breast halves (about 1¼ pounds)**
- 2 **tablespoons all-purpose flour**
- 2 **tablespoons salt-free Cajun seasoning**
- 1 **tablespoon vegetable oil**
- 2 **cups heavy cream**
- 2 **cups shredded Cheddar and Monterey Jack cheese blend (8 ounces)**
- ½ **teaspoon salt**
- 3 **cups seeded, diced tomatoes (3 large)**
- ¼ **cup sliced scallions (2)**
   Hot-pepper sauce, for serving (optional)

1. Cook pasta following package directions. Drain well; return pasta to pan.

2. Cut chicken into 1-inch pieces. In large food-storage bag, place chicken pieces, flour and 1 tablespoon of the Cajun seasoning; seal and toss to coat. Heat oil in large skillet over medium-high heat. Add chicken; cook and stir until chicken is no longer pink. Set chicken aside.

3. In medium-size saucepan, bring heavy cream just to a boil over medium heat, stirring occasionally. Remove from heat; whisk in 1 cup of the cheese, the remaining 1 tablespoon Cajun seasoning and the salt until cheese is melted and mixture is smooth.

4. In very large bowl, combine cooked pasta, cooked chicken, cream mixture, tomatoes and the remaining 1 cup cheese. Transfer mixture to greased 13×9×2-inch baking dish.

5. Bake, covered, at 350° for 25 to 30 minutes or until mixture is heated through. Sprinkle with scallions before serving. If desired, pass hot-pepper sauce at the table.

Make-ahead directions: Prepare casserole as directed through Step 4. Cover with plastic wrap, then foil, and refrigerate up to 24 hours. To serve, heat oven to 350°. Remove plastic wrap. Bake casserole, covered with foil, at 350° for 35 to 40 minutes or until mixture is heated through.

Per serving: 641 cal., 35 g total fat (20 g sat. fat), 151 mg chol., 448 mg sodium, 49 g carbo., 3 g fiber, 33 g pro.

Baked Cavatelli

Italian sausage generally comes "sweet" (another word for mild) or spicy. You can use either one in this dish, depending on the crowd you're feeding.

PREP: 25 minutes
BAKE: at 375° for 35 to 40 minutes
STAND: 10 minutes
MAKES: 8 main-dish servings

- 1 **pound cavatelli or wagon wheel macaroni (about 3½ cups)**
- 1 **pound uncooked Italian sausage links, sliced ½ inch thick, or lean ground beef**
- 1¼ **cups chopped onions**
- 3 **cloves garlic, minced**
- 2 **jars (26 ounces each) tomato pasta sauce**
- 1½ **cups shredded mozzarella cheese (6 ounces)**
- ¼ **teaspoon black pepper**

1. Heat oven to 375°. Cook pasta following package directions. Drain well; set aside.

2. In large skillet, cook sausage, onion and garlic over medium heat until meat is cooked through and onion is tender; drain off fat. Remove from skillet.

3. In very large bowl, stir together pasta sauce, 1 cup of the mozzarella cheese and the pepper. Add cooked pasta and meat mixture. Stir gently to combine. Spoon into ungreased 13×9×2-inch baking dish.

4. Bake, covered, at 375° for 30 to 35 minutes or until heated through. Uncover; sprinkle with the remaining ½ cup mozzarella cheese. Bake about 5 minutes or until cheese is melted. Let stand for 10 minutes before serving.

Per serving: 547 cal., 24 g total fat (9 g sat. fat), 57 mg chol., 1,130 mg sodium, 59 g carbo., 5 g fiber, 24 g pro.

Ham Balls in Barbecue Sauce

If you have a favorite bottled barbecue sauce or simply want to streamline this recipe a bit, you can use 1 cup of it in place of the sauce below.

PREP: 20 minutes
BAKE: 350° about 45 minutes
MAKES: 6 main-dish servings

Ham Balls:
- 2 eggs, lightly beaten
- 1½ cups soft bread crumbs (2 slices)
- ½ cup finely chopped onion (1 medium-size)
- 2 tablespoons milk
- 1 teaspoon dry mustard
- ¼ teaspoon black pepper
- ¾ pound ground cooked ham
- ¾ pound ground pork or ground beef

Barbecue Sauce:
- ¾ cup packed brown sugar
- ½ cup ketchup
- 2 tablespoons vinegar
- 1 teaspoon dry mustard

1. Ham Balls: Heat oven to 350°. In large bowl, combine eggs, bread crumbs, onion, milk, 1 teaspoon dry mustard and the pepper. Add ground ham and ground pork; mix well. Shape into 12 balls, using about ⅓ cup mixture for each. Place ham balls in a lightly greased 12×8×2-inch baking dish.

2. Barbecue Sauce: In small bowl, combine brown sugar, ketchup, vinegar and 1 teaspoon dry mustard. Stir until sugar is dissolved. Pour over meatballs.

3. Bake, uncovered, at 350° about 45 minutes or until internal temperature registers 160° on an instant-read meat thermometer inserted into meatballs. Transfer meatballs and sauce to a serving platter to serve.

Per serving: 427 cal., 19 g total fat (7 g sat. fat), 143 mg chol., 1,107 mg sodium, 42 g carbo., 1 g fiber, 23 g pro.

Chapter 8

Finger Food

In some situations, fork-free eating is the only way to go—for movie night at home, watching the big game or picnicking in the park. These recipes require no flatware but guarantee great taste.

New Orleans-Style Muffuletta

The Caribbean Grill

One of the esteemed judges of the 2004 Search for the Greatest Grilled Cheese Sandwich in America sponsored by DuPont® deemed Ashley Berman's entry as not only tasting great, but also as "extremely creative." Ashley, of New York City, went home from the contest with the $10,000 grand prize and a trip to California's Sonoma County cheese country.

PREP: 20 minutes
COOK: 4 minutes
MAKES: 4 sandwiches

Mango Salsa:
- ½ of a ripe mango, finely chopped
- ¼ cup finely chopped sweet red pepper
- 2 tablespoons finely chopped red onion
- 1 tablespoon lime juice
- ¼ teaspoon kosher salt
- ⅛ teaspoon sugar
- ⅛ teaspoon freshly ground black pepper

Sandwiches:
- 3 tablespoons butter, softened
- 1 tablespoon curry powder
- ¼ cup honey mustard
- 8 slices Italian bread
- 8 slices (1 ounce each) Swiss cheese

1. Mango Salsa: In small bowl, combine mango, sweet pepper, onion, lime juice, salt, sugar and black pepper; set aside. (This can be made a day ahead and refrigerated; bring to room temperature before serving.)

2. Sandwiches: In small bowl, stir together the softened butter and curry powder; set aside. Spread mustard on one side of all the bread slices. Spoon salsa on 4 of the bread slices. Top with 2 slices cheese, folding cheese to fit. Place the remaining 4 bread slices on top, mustard sides down. Spread tops of sandwiches with 1 tablespoon of the curry butter.

3. In very large skillet, heat 1 tablespoon curry butter over medium heat until hot. Add sandwiches to skillet, butter sides down. Carefully spread unbuttered bread with remaining 1 tablespoon curry butter. Cook for 2 to 3 minutes, or until undersides are golden brown and cheese begins to melt. Turn sandwiches; press down on them firmly with metal spatula. Cook for 2 to 3 minutes more or until golden brown and the cheese has melted. Turn once more; press with spatula and cook for 30 seconds. Cut sandwiches diagonally to serve.

Per sandwich: 497 cal., 27 g total fat (16 g sat. fat), 75 mg chol., 733 mg sodium, 43 g carbo., 3 g fiber, 21 g pro.

Cajun Chicken Pizza

The out-of-town hunters and tourists who find their way to David Smith's Pizza Palace Plus in Emporium, Pennsylvania, tell him his pizza is the best they've ever had. "I said to my wife, 'Let's go to a competition and see how good we really are,'" he says. Apparently, very good. His Cajun Chicken Pizza earned top prize at the 2007 American Pizza Championship.

PREP: 1 hour
MARINATE: 3 to 24 hours
RISE: 1 to 1½ hours
BAKE: at 450° for 15 to 20 minutes + 17 to 20 minutes
MAKES: 8 servings

- 1 package active dry yeast
- 1 cup warm water (120° to 130°)
- ½ teaspoon salt
- 2¾ to 3¼ cups bread flour (General Mills® Harvest King® works well)
- 1 tablespoon olive oil
- ½ cup Cajun Sauce (see recipe, far right)
- 3 cups shredded mozzarella and/or provolone cheese (12 ounces)
  Cajun Chicken (see recipe, far right)
- 8 strips bacon, crisp-cooked, drained and crumbled (about ½ cup)
- 2 ribs celery, chopped (1 cup)
- ½ cup freshly grated Parmesan and/or Romano cheese
- 2 teaspoons dried oregano or basil
- ½ cup bottled blue cheese salad dressing

1. In large bowl, sprinkle yeast over warm water. Stir to dissolve. Stir in ½ teaspoon salt and 1 cup of the flour until mixture is smooth. Stir in as much of the remaining flour as you can with a wooden spoon.

2. Turn dough out onto a lightly floured surface. Knead in enough of the remaining flour to make a moderately stiff dough that is smooth and elastic (6 to 8 minutes total). Form dough into a ball. Brush inside of large bowl with 1 tablespoon oil. Place dough in bowl; turn to coat all sides of dough with the oil. Cover and let rise in a warm place until double (1 to 1½ hours).

3. Heat oven to 450°. Grease two 12- to 14-inch pizza pans; set aside. Punch dough down. Divide dough in half. Press each half into a prepared pizza pan. Bake at 450° for 5 minutes.

4. Spread ¼ cup Cajun Sauce evenly over each pizza crust, leaving a ½-inch border around edges. Top with mozzarella cheese, Cajun Chicken, bacon, celery, Parmesan cheese and oregano.

5. Bake at 450° for 12 to 15 minutes or until crust is golden brown and cheese is melted. Drizzle each pizza with ¼ cup of the blue cheese dressing. Cut each pizza into 8 pieces and serve.

Cajun Sauce:

- ¾ **cup ketchup**
- ¼ **cup plus 2 tablespoons strong brewed coffee**
- ¼ **cup packed dark-brown sugar**
- 3 **tablespoons Worcestershire sauce**
- 2 **teaspoons lemon juice**
- 1 **clove garlic, minced**
- ½ **teaspoon dried oregano**
- ½ **teaspoon dried rosemary**
- 1 **bay leaf**
- ½ **teaspoon paprika**
- ¼ **teaspoon cayenne pepper**
- ½ **teaspoon black pepper**
- ¼ **teaspoon salt**

1. In small saucepan, combine ketchup, coffee, brown sugar, Worcestershire sauce, lemon juice, garlic, oregano, rosemary, bay leaf, paprika, cayenne, black pepper and salt. Bring to a boil, stirring occasionally. Remove from heat; cool. Store leftover sauce in an airtight container in refrigerator up to 2 weeks. Makes 1½ cups.

Cajun Chicken:

- 3 **tablespoons soy sauce**
- ½ **teaspoon fajita seasoning**
- ½ **teaspoon Cajun seasoning**
- 2 **boneless, skinless chicken breast halves**
  Nonstick cooking spray

1. In large food-storage bag, combine soy sauce, fajita seasoning and Cajun seasoning. Add chicken to bag. Seal bag and turn to coat chicken. Marinate in the refrigerator for at least 3 hours or up to 24 hours, turning bag occasionally. Heat oven to 450°. Line 15×10×1-inch baking pan with foil; lightly coat foil with nonstick cooking spray. Drain chicken; discard marinade. Place chicken in prepared pan. Bake at 450° for 15 to 20 minutes or until chicken is no longer pink (170°). Cool chicken slightly; chop chicken. (Chicken can be baked ahead. Place baked and chopped chicken in an airtight container and store in the refrigerator up to 24 hours.)

Per serving: 518 cal., 25 g total fat (9 g sat. fat), 63 mg chol.,1161 mg sodium, 43 g carbo., 2 g fiber, 32 g pro.

Chorizo-Topped Mexican Pizzas

You'll know if an avocado is ripe if it yields slightly to gentle pressure. The best way to pit one is by slipping a spoon underneath the seed and simply popping it out from the flesh.

PREP: 20 minutes
BROIL: 2 to 3 minutes
MAKES: 4 individual pizzas

½ **pound chorizo sausage**
1 **cup deli-fresh chunky salsa with corn and beans**
  Nonstick cooking spray
4 **(7- to 8-inch) flour tortillas**
1 **cup shredded Mexican cheese blend (4 ounces)**
1 **avocado, halved, pitted, peeled and sliced**
½ **cup chopped scallions (4)**
¼ **cup chopped fresh cilantro leaves**
  Lime wedges, for serving (optional)

1. Preheat broiler. In large skillet, crumble and cook chorizo over medium heat until no pink remains. Drain in colander. In small saucepan, heat salsa over medium heat until heated through.

2. Lightly coat large baking sheet with nonstick cooking spray. Arrange tortillas, two at a time, on baking sheet; top each with ¼ cup of the cheese. Broil 3 to 4 inches from heat for 2 to 3 minutes, until cheese is melted. Top each pizza with ¼ cup of the warm salsa, cooked chorizo, avocado, scallions and cilantro. If desired, serve with lime wedges.

Per pizza: 588 cal., 41 g total fat (15 g sat. fat), 75 mg chol., 1,242 mg sodium, 31 g carbo., 6 g fiber, 24 g pro.

Beef and Blue Pizza

With a total prep time of just 20 minutes, a piping-hot pizza can be on the table in less time than it takes to pick up the phone and call the delivery person.

PREP: 10 minutes
BAKE: at 425° for 5 minutes
BROIL: 4 to 5 minutes
MAKES: 4 servings

- ½ of a medium-size red onion, cut into thin slivers
- 2 tablespoons olive oil
- 1 (12-inch) baked pizza crust (such as Boboli)
- ½ pound thinly sliced cooked roast beef
- 1 small green or sweet red pepper, seeded and chopped
- 1 cup crumbled blue cheese (4 ounces)
- ¼ teaspoon pizza seasoning (optional)

1. Position oven rack in the center of the oven. Heat oven to 425°. In large skillet, cook onion in 1 tablespoon of the olive oil over medium-high heat for 3 to 5 minutes or just until onion is tender.

2. Place pizza crust on large baking sheet; brush with remaining 1 tablespoon olive oil. Bake at 425° for 5 minutes. Change oven setting to broil.

3. Place beef on cutting board; layer the slices to make a stack, if necessary. Slice beef crosswise into strips. Top pizza crust with beef, chopped pepper, cooked onion, blue cheese and, if desired, pizza seasoning.

4. Broil pizza for 4 to 5 minutes or until toppings are heated through and crust is lightly browned. Cut in wedges to serve.

Per serving: 553 cal., 23 g total fat (7 g sat. fat), 56 mg chol., 1,637 mg sodium, 54 g carbo., 1 g fiber, 31 g pro.

Spicy Reuben Melts

The "spicy" in these sandwiches comes from lip-twisting pepperoncini salad peppers. Briefly rinse them under cold water to lessen their salty, vinegary flavor, if you like.

PREP: 20 minutes
BROIL: 2 minutes
MAKES: 4 sandwiches

- 8 slices rye bread, toasted
- ½ pound sliced corned beef or pastrami
- ½ cup sauerkraut, rinsed and drained
- 12 bottled pepperoncini salad peppers, sliced
- 4 slices Swiss cheese
- ¼ cup bottled Thousand Island salad dressing

1. Preheat broiler. Place 4 bread slices on a baking sheet. Top the bread slices with corned beef, sauerkraut, pepperoncini and cheese. Broil 4 to 5 inches from the heat about 2 minutes or until cheese melts. Spread salad dressing on remaining 4 bread slices. Place bread, dressing side down, on top of broiled sandwiches.

2. Cut each sandwich in half and serve immediately.

Per sandwich: 394 cal., 17 g total fat (6 g sat. fat), 55 mg chol., 2,056 mg sodium, 38 g carbo., 5 g fiber, 24 g pro.

Italian Sausage Grinders

Grinders are great street food. Enjoy them at home—piping hot and saucy, with lots of napkins at hand—and for a much better price than you'd pay at the fair.

PREP: 25 minutes
COOK: 30 minutes
BROIL: 2 to 3 minutes
MAKES: 4 sandwiches

- 1 pound bulk hot or sweet Italian sausage
- 1 can (15 ounces) fire-roasted diced tomatoes
- 1 can (15 ounces) crushed tomatoes
- 2 cloves garlic, minced
- 1 teaspoon balsamic vinegar
- 1 teaspoon dried basil
- ½ teaspoon dried oregano
- ¼ teaspoon salt
- ¼ teaspoon red pepper flakes
- 1 small yellow onion, sliced
- 1 small green pepper, seeded and cut into strips
- 2 tablespoons olive oil
- 4 French-style rolls or hoagie buns, split
- 4 slices provolone cheese

1. In large saucepan, cook the sausage over medium heat until no longer pink; drain off fat. Stir in undrained diced tomatoes, undrained crushed tomatoes, garlic, vinegar, basil, oregano, salt and red pepper flakes. Bring to a boil; reduce heat. Simmer, uncovered, about 30 minutes or until mixture is thickened.

2. While sausage mixture cooks, in large skillet, cook onion and green pepper in hot olive oil over medium heat until tender. Set aside and keep warm.

3. Preheat broiler. Place rolls on baking sheet. Spoon sausage mixture on bottom halves of the rolls. Top with the onion mixture and cheese. Broil 4 to 5 inches from the heat for 2 to 3 minutes or until cheese is melted.

Per sandwich: 663 cal., 42 g total fat (16 g sat. fat), 96 mg chol., 1820 mg sodium, 35 g carbo., 4 g fiber, 29 g pro.

Variation: If desired, omit onion, green pepper and olive oil. Top meat mixture evenly with ½ cup bottled roasted sweet red peppers, drained, and ½ cup bottled sliced banana or pepperoncini peppers, drained.

Pepper Stromzoni

A kind of cross between a calzone (a half-moon-shaped pizza turnover) and a stromboli (a rolled pizza), this vegetarian stuffed pizza is as fun to make as it is to eat.

PREP: 30 minutes
BAKE: at 400° for 15 to 18 minutes
STAND: 10 minutes
MAKES: 4 servings

- 3 medium-size sweet red, sweet yellow and/or green peppers, chopped (3 cups)
- 6 cloves garlic, minced
- 1 tablespoon butter
- ½ teaspoon salt
- ¼ teaspoon black pepper
- ¼ to ½ teaspoon red pepper flakes
- ¾ cup shredded mozzarella cheese (3 ounces)
- ½ cup ricotta cheese
- 2 tablespoons chopped fresh basil leaves
- 1 tube (13.8 ounces) refrigerated pizza dough
- 1 egg, lightly beaten

1. Heat oven to 400°. Line large baking sheet with foil or parchment paper; grease foil. In large skillet, cook peppers and garlic in hot butter over medium heat 5 minutes or until tender, stirring occasionally. Stir in salt, black pepper and red pepper flakes; set aside.

2. In medium-size bowl, stir together the mozzarella cheese, ricotta cheese and basil. Stir cooked pepper mixture into cheese mixture until well combined; set aside.

3. On lightly floured surface, roll out dough to 16×10-inch rectangle. Cut into two 10×8-inch rectangles. Spoon half of the cheese mixture along one of the long sides of one rectangle, leaving a 1-inch border along the long side and a ½-inch border along the short sides. Spread to a width of 3 inches. Fold one long side over mixture. Seal seam and ends, tucking seam under loaf. Place on prepared baking sheet. Repeat with remaining dough and filling.

4. With a sharp knife cut 4 diagonal slits in the top of each loaf. Brush loaves with egg. Bake at 400° for 15 to 18 minutes or until golden brown. Let stand for 10 minutes. Slice each in half and serve warm.

Per serving: 365 cal., 14 g total fat (7 g sat. fat), 89 mg chol., 855 mg sodium, 42 g carbo., 3 g fiber, 17 g pro.

Pulled Chicken Sandwiches

Shredded meat from a rotisserie chicken is tossed with a simple barbecue sauce to make a speedy dinner that tastes like it's been simmered and slow cooked, but hasn't.

PREP: 25 minutes
COOK: 7 minutes
MAKES: 4 sandwiches

- 1 rotisserie chicken (2 to 2¼ pounds)
- 1 tablespoon olive oil
- 1 medium-size onion, sliced ¼ inch thick
- ⅓ cup cider vinegar or white wine vinegar
- ½ cup tomato sauce
- 3 to 4 tablespoons seeded and finely chopped fresh red and/or green hot chiles*
- 2 tablespoons chopped fresh thyme leaves
- 2 tablespoons molasses
- 2 tablespoons water
- ½ teaspoon salt
- 4 sandwich buns, split
  Bread-and-butter pickle slices

1. Remove meat from chicken (discard skin and bones). With two forks or your fingers, pull meat into shreds.

2. In large skillet, heat olive oil over medium heat. Add onion; cook about 5 minutes or until tender, stirring occasionally to separate into rings. Add vinegar; cook and stir for 1 minute more.

3. Stir in tomato sauce, chiles, thyme, molasses, water and salt. Bring to a boil. Add the chicken; toss gently to coat. Heat through. Serve chicken mixture in buns with pickle slices.

*Note: Hot chiles contain oils that can burn your skin and eyes. Avoid direct contact with them as much as possible. When working with hot chiles, wear plastic or rubber gloves. If your bare hands do touch chiles, wash your hands with soap and warm water.

Per sandwich: 445 cal., 12 g total fat (3 g sat. fat), 84 mg chol., 990 mg sodium, 51 g carbo., 2 g fiber, 33 g pro.

Gyro Sandwiches

Get the taste of an authentic Greek gyro at home. These savory sandwiches feature a perfectly seasoned lamb patty wrapped up in a warm pita and dressed with tomato, feta cheese and a creamy cucumber-mint sauce.

PREP: 25 minutes
BROIL: 10 to 12 minutes
MAKES: 4 sandwiches

- 1 pound ground lamb or beef
- 2 teaspoons dried minced onion
- 1 teaspoon garlic powder
- 1 teaspoon Greek seasoning or dried oregano
- ½ teaspoon salt
- ¼ teaspoon black pepper
- 1 container (6 ounces) plain low-fat yogurt or ⅔ cup sour cream
- ¼ cup chopped, seeded cucumber
- 2 teaspoons chopped fresh mint or Italian (flat-leaf) parsley leaves
- 1 clove garlic, minced
- 4 soft pita bread rounds, warmed*
- 1 medium-size tomato, thinly sliced
- ¼ cup thinly slivered red onion
- ⅓ cup crumbled feta cheese

1. Preheat broiler. In medium-size bowl, combine lamb, onion, garlic powder, Greek seasoning, salt and pepper. Shape into four ½-inch-thick oval patties. Place on unheated rack of a broiler pan.

2. Broil patties 4 to 5 inches from heat for 10 to 12 minutes or until internal temperature registers 160° on an instant-read meat thermometer inserted in centers of patties. Turn patties over once, halfway through broiling.

3. Meanwhile, in small bowl, stir together yogurt, cucumber, mint and garlic; set aside.

4. To serve, layer pitas with tomato, yogurt mixture, red onion, feta cheese and patties; fold pitas over patties.

*Note: To warm pitas, wrap in microwave-safe paper towels. Microwave on 100% power (high) about 1 minute.

Per sandwich: 462 cal., 20 g total fat (9 g sat. fat), 89 mg chol., 868 mg sodium, 41 g carbo., 2 g fiber, 29 g pro.

Mexi-Pork Wraps

These fresh and flavorful wraps go together so quickly, you can steer clear of your local fast-food Mexican place—and the less-than-healthful fare found there.

START TO FINISH: 35 minutes
MAKES: 4 wraps

- 8 ounces lean boneless pork, cut into thin bite-size strips
- 1 clove garlic, minced
- 1 tablespoon olive oil
- ¾ cup frozen whole kernel corn, thawed
- ½ cup chopped roasted sweet red peppers
- ¼ cup sliced scallions (2)
- 3 tablespoons lime juice
- ½ teaspoon ground cumin
- ⅛ teaspoon cayenne pepper (optional)
- ½ cup refried black beans*
- 4 (9- or 10-inch) whole-grain tortillas
- ½ cup shredded romaine lettuce
- ½ cup chopped tomato (1 medium-size)
  Light sour cream (optional)

1. In large skillet, cook and stir pork strips and garlic in hot olive oil over medium-high heat for 4 to 5 minutes or until no pink remains; set aside.

2. In medium-size bowl, stir together corn, peppers, scallions, 2 tablespoons of the lime juice, cumin and, if desired, cayenne pepper. In small bowl, stir together refried beans and the remaining 1 tablespoon lime juice.

3. Spread 2 tablespoons of the bean mixture in 2-inch-wide strip down center of each tortilla. Top with pork strips, corn mixture, romaine and tomato. Fold bottom edge of each tortilla up and over the filling. Roll up tortillas around filling. If desired, serve wraps with sour cream.

*Note: If you can't find refried black beans, rinse and drain ½ of a can (15 ounces) black beans. In small bowl, mash beans; stir in the 1 tablespoon lime juice.

Per wrap: 316 cal., 11 g total fat (3 g sat. fat), 36 mg chol., 484 mg sodium, 39 g carbo., 5 g fiber, 17 g pro.

Mexi-Chicken Wraps: Prepare as above, except substitute boneless, skinless chicken breast halves, cut into bite-size strips, for the pork.

Thai Pork Roll-Ups

If you like your peanut sauce with some kick to it, add ¼ teaspoon red pepper flakes to the sauce as you stir and heat it.

PREP: 25 minutes
BAKE: at 350° about 10 minutes
MAKES: 6 wraps

- 6 (8- to 10-inch) spinach, tomato and/or plain flour tortillas
- ½ teaspoon garlic salt
- ¼ to ½ teaspoon black pepper
- 1 pork tenderloin (¾ pound), cut into 1-inch strips
- 1 tablespoon vegetable oil
- 4 cups packaged shredded broccoli (broccoli slaw mix)
- 1 medium-size red onion, cut into thin wedges
- 1 teaspoon grated fresh ginger

Peanut Sauce:
- ¼ cup creamy peanut butter
- 3 tablespoons water
- 1 tablespoon sugar
- 2 teaspoons soy sauce
- 1 clove garlic, minced

1. Heat oven to 350°. Wrap tortillas in foil. Bake at 350° about 10 minutes or until warm.

2. While tortillas are warming, in medium-size bowl, combine garlic salt and pepper. Add pork, tossing to coat evenly. In large skillet, cook and stir pork in hot oil over medium-high heat for 4 to 6 minutes or until no longer pink. Turn heat down if pork gets too brown. Remove pork from skillet; keep warm. Add broccoli, onion and ginger to skillet. Cook and stir for 4 to 6 minutes or until vegetables are crisp-tender. Remove from heat; keep warm.

3. Peanut Sauce: In small saucepan, combine peanut butter, water, sugar, soy sauce and garlic. Heat over medium-low heat, whisking constantly, until mixture is smooth and warm.

4. To assemble, spread one side of each tortilla with Peanut Sauce. Top with pork strips and vegetable mixture. Roll up each tortilla, securing with a wooden toothpick. Serve immediately.

Thai Chicken Roll-Ups: Prepare as directed above, except substitute 12 ounces boneless, skinless chicken breast halves, cut into strips, for the pork.

Per wrap: 389 cal., 13 g total fat (3 g sat. fat), 37 mg chol., 649 mg sodium, 44 g carbo., 5 g fiber, 22 g pro.

Caribbean Crab Wraps

These quick-to-fix, totable wraps make a great weekday lunch. If you take one to the office, just be sure you store it in the refrigerator or in an insulated container outfitted with a freezer pack.

START TO FINISH: 25 minutes
MAKES: 3 wraps

- 1 package (8 ounces) chunk-style imitation crabmeat, flaked
- 1 medium-size zucchini (8 ounces), shredded
- 1 cup coarsely chopped, peeled fresh pineapple
- ¼ cup chopped scallions (2)
- 2 tablespoons canned diced green chiles
- ½ teaspoon salt
- ¼ teaspoon black pepper
- 6 tablespoons tub-style cream cheese spread with chive and onion
- 3 (10-inch) tomato-flavor flour tortillas
- ⅓ cup shredded coconut, toasted

1. In large bowl, toss together crabmeat, zucchini, pineapple, scallions, chiles, salt and black pepper. Set aside.

2. Spread 2 tablespoons cream cheese over one side of each tortilla. Arrange crabmeat mixture over the cream cheese. Sprinkle with coconut. Roll up.

Per wrap: 386 cal., 18 g total fat (11 g sat. fat), 45 mg chol., 1591 mg sodium, 49 g carbo., 15 g fiber, 17 g pro.

New Orleans-Style Muffuletta

The signature sandwich of the Crescent City, the picnic-perfect muffuletta was invented in 1906 at the Italian-owned Central Grocery in New Orleans. Another name for the pickled mixed vegetables is giardiniera—and it can be found in varying degress of hotness.

START TO FINISH: 30 minutes
MAKES: 6 servings

- 1 jar (16 ounces) pickled mixed vegetables
- ¼ cup chopped pimiento-stuffed green olives and/or pitted ripe olives
- 1 clove garlic, minced
- 1 tablespoon olive oil
- 1 loaf (16 ounces) ciabatta or unsliced French bread
- 6 lettuce leaves
- 3 ounces thinly sliced salami, pepperoni or summer sausage
- 3 ounces thinly sliced cooked ham or turkey
- 6 ounces thinly sliced provolone, Swiss or mozzarella cheese
- 1 to 2 medium-size tomatoes, thinly sliced
- ⅛ teaspoon coarsely ground black pepper

1. Drain vegetables, reserving 2 tablespoons liquid. Chop vegetables. Combine vegetables, reserved liquid, olives, garlic and olive oil. Set aside.

2. Split the loaf of bread in half lengthwise. Hollow out inside of the top half, leaving a ¾-inch-thick shell.

3. Top the bottom bread half with lettuce leaves, desired meats, desired cheese and tomato slices. Sprinkle tomato slices with pepper. Stir vegetable mixture; mound on top of tomato slices. Top with hollowed-out bread half. To serve, slice into 6 portions.

Per serving: 440 cal., 17 g total fat (8 g sat. fat), 41 mg chol., 2246 mg sodium, 48 g carbo., 3 g fiber, 23 g pro.

Chapter 9

Sweet Endings

Save room for dessert. These sweet indulgences range from simple bars to spectacular special-occasion creations—from a warm bread pudding to a fabulous frozen peppermint-fudge pie.

Rhubarb Surprise Crisp

Apple Yum Crumb Pie

Evette Rahman of Orlando, Florida, achieved pie perfection with her first-place winner in the amateur division of the 2008 American Pie Council®/Crisco National Pie Championships. She used a mix of McIntosh and Golden Delicious apples and came up with a pie that pleased crumb and crust lovers alike. "I thought, 'Why not have the best of both worlds?' " she says.

PREP: 40 minutes
BAKE: at 400° for 20 minutes and at 375° for 35 minutes
CHILL: 1 hour
MAKES: 8 servings

Pastry:
- 2 cups all-purpose flour
- 2 tablespoons granulated sugar
- 1 teaspoon salt
- ½ teaspoon baking powder
- ⅓ cup Crisco® solid vegetable shortening
- ⅓ cup very cold unsalted butter, cubed
- 1 tablespoon vegetable oil
- 1 tablespoon vinegar
- ⅓ cup heavy cream

Filling:
- 7 cups peeled, cored and sliced cooking apples
- 1½ tablespoons butter, melted
- ¾ cup plus 2 tablespoons granulated sugar
- ¼ cup cornstarch
- ½ teaspoon plus ⅛ teaspoon ground cinnamon
- ¼ teaspoon freshly grated nutmeg
- 1 egg, lightly beaten
- 1 tablespoon sliced almonds
  Granulated sugar, for sprinkling

Topping:
- ½ cup all-purpose flour
- ¼ cup packed light-brown sugar
- ¼ teaspoon ground cinnamon
  Dash salt
- ¼ cup very cold unsalted butter, cubed
  Sliced almonds (optional)

Icing:
- ¼ cup confectioners' sugar
- 1½ teaspoons milk
  Dash of vanilla extract

1. Pastry: In medium-size bowl, combine 2 cups flour, 2 tablespoons granulated sugar, 1 teaspoon salt and the baking powder. With pastry blender, cut in shortening and ⅓ cup butter until pieces are pea-size. Stir together oil, vinegar and cream. Gradually add to flour mixture. Knead dough lightly. Form into 2 disks. Wrap separately in plastic wrap and refrigerate for at least 1 hour.

2. On lightly floured surface, roll out one portion of dough. Line 9- or 10-inch pie plate with pastry; set aside.

3. Filling: In large bowl, toss apples with 1½ tablespoons melted butter. Add ¾ cup plus 2 tablespoons granulated sugar, cornstarch, ½ teaspoon plus ⅛ teaspoon cinnamon and nutmeg. Gently stir until combined. Transfer filling to pastry-lined pie plate.

4. Roll out the remaining dough; place on filling. Cut 6 evenly spaced 3×1½-inch rectangles in top pastry, starting from the edge of the pie and moving toward center. Cut a small round hole in center. Crimp edges. In small bowl, whisk together egg and 1 teaspoon water. Brush dough with egg mixture and the 1 tablespoon almonds and sprinkle with sugar.

5. Heat oven to 400°. Freeze pie for 15 minutes. Cut six 3×1½-inch pieces of parchment paper. Cover rectangular holes with the parchment. Cover edge of pie with foil to prevent overbrowning. Place pie on baking sheet. Bake pie at 400° for 20 minutes. Remove foil. Reduce oven temperature to 375°; bake at 375° for 10 minutes.

6. Topping: In medium-size bowl, combine ½ cup flour, brown sugar, ¼ teaspoon cinnamon and a dash salt. With pastry blender, cut in ¼ cup butter until fine crumbs form. Remove pie from oven; remove parchment. Carefully spoon approximately 1 tablespoon topping into each hole. (Freeze any leftover topping for another use.) If desired, place several almond slices in each of the openings.

7. Return pie to the oven and bake at 375° for 25 to 35 minutes more or until golden brown. Cool completely on wire rack.

8. Icing: In small bowl, stir together confectioners' sugar, milk and vanilla. Drizzle over pie.

Per serving: 623 cal., 31 g total fat (15 g sat. fat), 82 mg chol., 364 mg sodium, 83 g carbo., 3 g fiber, 6 g pro.

Warm, Sticky Toffee Cake

Beth Royals of Richmond, Virginia, so successfully streamlined one of her favorite dessert recipes, it won first prize in the dessert division of the Family Circle 75th Anniversary recipe contest. Based on a popular English dessert—sticky toffee pudding—her cake relies on a combination of caramel topping and cream as stand-in for homemade caramel sauce.

PREP: 15 minutes
BAKE: at 350° about 37 minutes
MAKES: 12 servings

	Nonstick cooking spray
1	package (8 ounces) pitted dates
1¼	cups water
1	box (18 ounces) yellow cake mix
1	container (6 ounces) vanilla yogurt
⅓	cup vegetable oil
3	large eggs
1	squeeze bottle (20 ounces) caramel ice-cream topping
2	tablespoons heavy cream
1	quart vanilla ice cream
	Fresh mint sprigs, for garnish (optional)

1. Heat oven to 350°. Coat 13×9×2-inch baking pan with nonstick cooking spray.

2. In medium-size bowl, combine dates and water; cover loosely with plastic wrap. Microwave on 100% power (high) for 4 minutes. Cool slightly. Transfer date mixture to food processor or blender; cover and process or blend until smooth. Set aside.

3. In large mixing bowl, combine cake mix, yogurt, oil and eggs. Beat with electric mixer on medium-high speed for 2 minutes. Add date puree; beat to combine. Pour into prepared pan.

4. Bake at 350° about 37 minutes or until wooden toothpick inserted in center comes out clean. Place cake on wire rack.

5. In small bowl, stir together caramel topping and heavy cream. Pour 1 cup caramel mixture over baked cake, spreading to edges. Cool cake 20 minutes. If desired, pour remaining caramel mixture back into squeeze bottle.

6. If desired, drizzle additional caramel topping onto dessert plates. Place a piece of cake and a scoop of ice cream on each plate. If desired, garnish with mint.

Per serving: 563 cal., 17 g total fat (6 g sat. fat), 78 mg chol., 471 mg sodium, 99 g carbo., 2 g fiber, 5 g pro.

Warm, Sticky Toffee Cake

Mixed Berry Cream Pie

A sour cream sauce poured on top of the berries before the crumb crust is sprinkled on makes this pie the best of both worlds—fruity and creamy.

PREP: 40 minutes
BAKE: at 450° for 13 to 14 minutes and at 375° about 50 minutes
CHILL: 3 hours
MAKES: 8 servings

Baked Pastry Shell:
1¼ **cups all-purpose flour**
¼ **teaspoon salt**
⅓ **cup solid vegetable shortening**
4 **to 5 tablespoons cold water**

Berry Filling:
6 **cups fresh blackberries, blueberries and/or raspberries***
1 **cup granulated sugar**
2 **tablespoons all-purpose flour**
1 **tablespoon lemon juice**
1 **carton (8 ounces) sour cream**
3 **tablespoons all-purpose flour**
¼ **teaspoon salt**

Crumb Topping:
½ **cup fine dry bread crumbs**
3 **tablespoons packed brown sugar**
2 **tablespoons (¼ stick) butter, melted**

1. Baked Pastry Shell: Heat oven to 450°. In large bowl, stir together 1¼ cups flour and ¼ teaspoon salt. With pastry blender, cut in shortening until pieces are pea-size. Sprinkle 1 tablespoon water over part of the flour mixture; gently toss with a fork. Push moistened dough to the side of the bowl. Repeat moistening mixture, using 1 tablespoon water at a time, until all dough is moistened. Form dough into a ball. On lightly floured surface, use your hands to flatten dough. Roll dough into 12-inch circle. Wrap pastry around the rolling pin. Unroll pastry into a 9-inch pie plate. Ease pastry into pie plate. Trim to ½ inch beyond edge of pie plate. Fold under extra pastry. Crimp edge as desired. Generously prick bottom and sides of pastry in pie plate with a fork. Prick all around where bottom and sides meet. Line pastry with a double thickness of foil. Bake at 450° for 8 minutes. Remove foil. Bake for 5 to 6 minutes more or until golden. Cool on a wire rack.

2. Berry Filling: Reduce oven temperature to 375°. In large bowl, toss berries with ¼ cup of the granulated sugar, 2 tablespoons flour and lemon juice. Transfer berry mixture to baked pastry shell. In medium-size bowl, combine sour cream, remaining ¾ cup granulated sugar, 3 tablespoons flour and ¼ teaspoon salt. Spread sour cream mixture over berries.

3. Crumb Topping: In small bowl, combine bread crumbs, brown sugar and melted butter. Sprinkle crumb mixture over sour cream mixture.

4. Cover edge of pie with foil. Place pie on baking sheet. Bake at 375° about 50 minutes or until juices are clear. Cool completely on wire rack; refrigerate for at least 3 hours before serving.

*Note: Do not use more than 3 cups raspberries in the berry mixture. Because raspberries are very juicy, using more than 3 cups may make the crust soggy.

Per serving: 463 cal., 23 g total fat (10 g sat. fat), 47 mg chol., 361 mg sodium, 62 g carbo., 7 g fiber, 5 g pro.

Brownie-Walnut Pie

This is like your favorite restaurant dessert—only better. A rich, fudgy brownie is the filling for this pie. Serve it à la mode, if you like, with a scoop of coffee or vanilla ice cream and a drizzle of caramel sauce.

PREP: 10 minutes
BAKE: at 350° for 50 to 55 minutes
COOL: 1 hour plus 20 minutes
MAKES: 10 to 12 servings

½ cup (1 stick) butter
3 ounces unsweetened chocolate, cut up
3 eggs, lightly beaten
1½ cups granulated sugar
½ cup all-purpose flour
1 teaspoon vanilla extract
1 cup chopped walnuts
1 9-inch unbaked pastry shell
Vanilla or coffee ice cream, for serving (optional)
Caramel ice-cream topping, for serving (optional)

1. In heavy, small saucepan, melt butter and chocolate over low heat, stirring frequently. Cool for 20 minutes.

2. Heat oven to 350°. In large bowl, stir together eggs, granulated sugar, flour and vanilla. Stir in cooled chocolate mixture and walnuts. Pour into pastry shell.

3. Bake at 350° for 50 to 55 minutes or until a knife inserted near the center comes out clean. Cool on wire rack for 1 hour. Serve warm. If desired, top with ice cream and drizzle with caramel topping.

Per serving: 458 cal., 28 g total fat (12 g sat. fat), 90 mg chol., 175 mg sodium, 50 g carbo., 2 g fiber, 6 g pro.

Peppermint-Fudge Pie

Spectacular and sweet, this festive frozen treat is perfect for a holiday celebration. Better yet, it can be made up to a day ahead of serving.

PREP: 50 minutes
BAKE: at 375° for 7 to 8 minutes and at 475° for 3 to 4 minutes
FREEZE: 14 to 32 hours
MAKES: 12 servings

Chocolate Crumb Crust:
Nonstick cooking spray
1 **cup very finely crushed vanilla wafers (about 22 cookies)**
⅓ **cup confectioners' sugar**
3 **tablespoons unsweetened cocoa powder**
3 **tablespoons butter, melted**

Fudge Sauce:
1 **cup granulated sugar**
1 **can (5 ounces) evaporated milk (⅔ cup)**
2 **tablespoons (¼ stick) butter**
2 **ounces unsweetened chocolate, cut up**
1 **teaspoon vanilla extract**
2 **pints (4 cups) peppermint ice cream**

Meringue:
¾ **cup granulated sugar**
½ **cup boiling water**
¼ **cup meringue powder**
10 **striped round peppermint candies, crushed (¼ cup)**

1. Chocolate Crumb Crust: Heat oven to 375°. Lightly coat 8-inch springform pan with nonstick cooking spray; set aside. In medium-size bowl, combine crushed vanilla wafers, confectioners' sugar and cocoa powder. Stir in 3 tablespoons melted butter. Pat crumb mixture firmly into the bottom of the prepared pan. Bake at 375° for 7 to 8 minutes or until crust is firm. Cool in pan on a wire rack.

2. Fudge Sauce: In small saucepan, combine the 1 cup granulated sugar, evaporated milk, 2 tablespoons butter and chocolate. Cook and stir over medium heat until bubbly; reduce heat. Boil gently for 4 to 5 minutes or until mixture is reduced to 1½ cups, stirring occasionally. Remove from heat; stir in vanilla. Beat until smooth with wire whisk. Set aside to cool completely.

3. In chilled medium-size bowl, stir 1 pint of the peppermint ice cream until softened. Spread over cooled crust. Dollop small spoonfuls of half of the cooled fudge sauce over the ice cream. Freeze 2 hours or until nearly firm. Repeat with remaining ice cream and fudge sauce. Return to freezer while preparing meringue.

4. Meringue: In medium-size bowl, dissolve sugar in boiling water. Cool to room temperature. Add meringue powder. Beat with electric mixer on low speed until combined; beat on high speed until stiff peaks form (tips stand straight). With wooden spoon, fold 3 tablespoons of the candy into meringue. Spread meringue over pie, sealing to edge. Freeze 6 hours or until firm.

5. Heat oven to 475°. Bake at 475° for 3 to 4 minutes or just until meringue is lightly browned. Cover loosely with foil. Freeze for at least 6 hours or up to 24 hours before serving. Sprinkle with remaining crushed candy.

Per serving: 385 cal., 15 g total fat (9 g sat. fat), 36 mg chol., 131 mg sodium, 61 g carbo., 1 g fiber, 4 g pro.

Rustic Peach Tart

Right before serving, sprinkle the tart with a few tablespoons of toasted sliced almonds, if you like.

PREP: 30 minutes
BAKE: at 375° for 35 to 45 minutes
COOL: 30 minutes
MAKES: 8 servings

- ¼ cup granulated sugar
- 4 teaspoons all-purpose flour
- 4 cups sliced, peeled fresh peaches or unsweetened frozen peach slices
- 1 tablespoon rum or lemon juice

Spiced Tart Pastry:
- 1¼ cups all-purpose flour
- ¼ teaspoon salt
- ⅛ teaspoon ground nutmeg
- ⅓ cup solid vegetable shortening
- 4 to 5 tablespoons cold water
- 1 egg, lightly beaten
- 1 tablespoon water
- Peach or apricot preserves, melted (optional)

Rum Whipped Cream:
- ½ cup heavy cream
- 2 teaspoons rum
- 1 teaspoon granulated sugar
- Sifted confectioners' sugar

1. In large bowl, stir together sugar and the 4 teaspoons flour. Add peaches and 1 tablespoon rum; toss gently until coated. If using frozen peaches, let stand 45 minutes or until fruit is partially thawed but still icy.

2. Spiced Tart Pastry: In medium-size bowl, stir together 1¼ cups flour, salt and nutmeg. With pastry blender, cut in shortening until pieces are pea-size. Sprinkle 1 tablespoon cold water over part of the flour mixture; gently toss with a fork. Push moistened pastry to the side of the bowl. Repeat moistening flour mixture using 1 tablespoon of water at a time, until all of the flour mixture is moistened. Form pastry into a ball. Line a large baking sheet with parchment paper or foil. Place pastry on prepared baking sheet; roll into a 13-inch circle. Set aside.

3. Heat oven to 375°. Mound peach mixture in center of pastry circle, leaving a 2-inch border. Fold border up over peaches, pleating pastry gently as needed. In small bowl, combine egg and 1 tablespoon water; brush onto the top and sides of the pastry.

4. Bake at 375° for 35 to 45 minutes or until pastry is golden and filling is bubbly. If necessary, to prevent overbrowning, cover edge of tart with foil the last 5 to 10 minutes of baking. If desired, brush filling with melted preserves. Cool on the baking sheet for 30 minutes.

5. Rum Whipped Cream: In chilled small mixing bowl, combine heavy cream, 2 teaspoons rum and 1 teaspoon granulated sugar. Beat with chilled beaters of an electric mixer on medium speed until soft peaks form (tips curl).

6. To serve, dust pastry edge with confectioners' sugar. Serve warm tart with Rum Whipped Cream.

Per serving: 279 cal., 15 g total fat (6 g sat. fat), 47 mg chol., 88 mg sodium, 32 g carbo., 2 g fiber, 4 g pro.

Chocolate Chip Oatmeal Cake

It's great to have a cake in your repertoire, like this one, that is so simple to fix, you can whip it up at a moment's notice. No frosting needed—just a pot of coffee or tea and some good company.

PREP: 25 minutes
STAND: 10 minutes
BAKE: at 350° for 40 minutes
COOL: 2 hours
MAKES: 20 servings

- 1 cup quick-cooking rolled oats
- 1¾ cups boiling water
- 1 cup granulated sugar
- 1 cup packed brown sugar
- ½ cup (1 stick) butter, cut up and softened
- 2 eggs
- 1¾ cups all-purpose flour
- 1 tablespoon unsweetened cocoa powder
- 1 teaspoon baking soda
- ½ teaspoon salt
- 1 package (12 ounces) semisweet chocolate chips (2 cups)
- ¾ cup chopped walnuts

1. Place oats in large bowl. Pour boiling water over the oats; let stand for 10 minutes. Grease and flour 13×9×2-inch baking pan; set aside.

2. Heat oven to 350°. Add granulated sugar, brown sugar and butter to oat mixture; stir until butter is melted. Stir in eggs until combined. Stir in flour, cocoa powder, baking soda and salt until combined. Stir in 1 cup of the chocolate chips. Pour batter into the prepared pan. Sprinkle with walnuts and the remaining chocolate chips.

3. Bake at 350° about 40 minutes or until wooden toothpick inserted near the center of cake comes out clean. Cool completely in pan on a wire rack.

Per serving: 297 cal., 13 g total fat (6 g sat. fat), 33 mg chol., 166 mg sodium, 38 g carbo., 3 g fiber, 2 g pro.

Crunchy Caramel Apple Cake

Use a good cooking apple that will keep its shape.

PREP: 30 minutes
BAKE: at 325° for 45 to 55 minutes
MAKES: 16 servings

Cake:
- 1 cup plain granola, crushed
- 1 cup chopped walnuts or pecans
- ¼ cup (½ stick) butter, softened
- 3 cups all-purpose flour
- 1 teaspoon baking soda
- 1 teaspoon ground cinnamon
- ½ teaspoon salt
- 2 eggs, lightly beaten
- 1½ cups vegetable oil
- 1 cup granulated sugar
- 1 cup packed brown sugar
- 3 cups finely chopped, peeled apples

Caramel Sauce:
- ½ cup (1 stick) butter
- 1 cup packed brown sugar
- ½ cup heavy cream
- 1 teaspoon vanilla extract

1. Cake: Heat oven to 325°. Grease 13×9×2-inch baking pan; set aside. In medium-size bowl, combine granola and ½ cup of the nuts. Combine ¼ cup softened butter with granola mixture until crumbly; set aside.

2. In medium-size bowl, stir together flour, baking soda, cinnamon and salt. In large bowl, stir together eggs, oil, granulated sugar and brown sugar. Add flour mixture; stir until combined. Fold in apples and remaining nuts. Spoon into pan; sprinkle with granola.

3. Bake at 325° for 45 to 55 minutes or until toothpick inserted in center comes out clean. Cool on a wire rack.

4. Caramel Sauce: In small saucepan, melt butter over medium heat. Stir in brown sugar and cream. Bring to a boil, stirring constantly; reduce heat. Simmer, uncovered, for 5 minutes or until slightly thickened. Stir in vanilla. Cool about 10 minutes. Serve warm with cake.

Per serving: 630 cal., 39 g total fat (10 g sat. fat), 61 mg chol., 240 mg sodium, 68 g carbo., 3 g fiber, 6 g pro.

Best-Ever Chocolate Cake

Natural or Dutch-process cocoa powder works here. Natural cocoa will give the cake a more intense flavor and darker color than the Dutch-process cocoa.

PREP: 50 minutes
STAND: 30 minutes
BAKE: 350° for 30 to 40 minutes
COOL: 15 minutes
MAKES: 12 to 16 servings

Cake:
- ¾ cup (1½ sticks) butter
- 3 eggs
- 2 cups all-purpose flour
- ¾ cup unsweetened cocoa powder
- 1 teaspoon baking soda
- ¾ teaspoon baking powder
- ½ teaspoon salt
- 2 cups sugar
- 2 teaspoons vanilla extract
- 1½ cups milk

Chocolate-Sour Cream Frosting:
- 1 package (12 ounces) semisweet chocolate chips
- ½ cup (1 stick) butter
- 1 carton (8 ounces) sour cream
- 4½ to 5 cups confectioners' sugar

1. Cake: Allow butter and eggs to stand at room temperature for 30 minutes. Heat oven to 350°. Grease bottoms of two 8×8×2-inch square or 9×1½-inch round cake pans. Line bottom of pans with waxed paper. Grease and lightly flour waxed paper and sides of pans. Or grease one 13×9×2-inch baking pan. Set pan(s) aside.

2. In medium-size bowl, stir together flour, cocoa powder, baking soda, baking powder and salt; set aside.

3. In large mixing bowl, beat butter with electric mixer on medium to high speed for 30 seconds. Add sugar, about ¼ cup at a time, beating on medium speed until well combined (3 to 4 minutes). Scrape sides of bowl; continue beating on medium speed for 2 minutes. Add eggs, one at a time, beating after each addition. Beat in vanilla.

4. Alternately add flour mixture and milk to beaten mixture, beating on low speed just until combined after each addition. Beat on medium to high speed for 20 seconds more. Spread batter evenly into the pan(s).

5. Bake layers at 350° for 35 to 40 minutes for 8-inch pans and the 13×9×2-inch pan, 30 to 35 minutes for 9-inch pans, or until wooden toothpick inserted near centers comes out clean. Cool in pans for 10 minutes. Remove from pans. Peel off waxed paper. Cool completely on wire racks. Or, place 13×9×2-inch cake in pan on a wire rack; cool.

6. Chocolate-Sour Cream Frosting: In large saucepan, melt chocolate chips and ½ cup butter over low heat, stirring frequently. Cool for 5 minutes. Stir in sour cream. Gradually add confectioners' sugar, beating with an electric mixer until smooth. Fill and frost layers or spread over 13×9-inch cake. Cover and store frosted cake in the refrigerator.

Per serving: 729 cal., 33 g total fat (19 g sat. fat), 115 mg chol., 394 mg sodium, 107 g carbo., 3 g fiber, 9 g pro.

Sugar-and-Spice Coffee Slices

The dough for these java-infused "icebox" cookies can be in the refrigerator at the ready for baking fresh for up to 3 days—or in the freezer for up to 1 week.

PREP: 25 minutes
BAKE: at 375° for 9 to 10 minutes per batch
CHILL: 2 hours
MAKES: about 4 dozen cookies

- ½ cup (1 stick) butter, softened
- ¼ cup solid vegetable shortening
- 1 cup granulated sugar
- ½ cup packed brown sugar
- 1 teaspoon baking powder
- 1 teaspoon ground cinnamon
- ¼ teaspoon salt
- 2 tablespoons instant espresso powder
- 1 tablespoon hot water
- 1 egg
- 2 cups all-purpose flour
- ¼ cup granulated sugar
- 1 teaspoon instant espresso powder
- Coffee beans (optional)

1. In large mixing bowl, beat butter and shortening with electric mixer on medium to high speed for 30 seconds. Add granulated sugar, brown sugar, baking powder, cinnamon and salt. Beat until combined, scraping sides of bowl occasionally. In small bowl, stir together 2 tablespoons espresso powder and the hot water until dissolved. Add to sugar mixture along with the egg; beat until combined. Beat in as much of the flour as you can with the mixer. With a wooden spoon, stir in remaining flour.

2. Divide dough into thirds. Shape each portion into a 7×2×1-inch loaf. Wrap each loaf in plastic wrap; refrigerate dough about 2 hours or until firm.*

3. Heat oven to 375°. Cut loaves into ⅜-inch slices. Place slices about 2 inches apart on ungreased cookie sheet. In small bowl, stir together ¼ cup granulated sugar and 1 teaspoon espresso powder. Sprinkle slices with sugar-espresso mixture. If desired, gently press a few coffee beans onto each slice.

4. Bake at 375° for 9 to 10 minutes or until edges are light brown. Let stand for 1 minute on cookie sheet. Transfer to wire rack; cool.

*Note: You can chill the dough loaves for up to 3 days in the refrigerator or freeze them for up to 1 week before slicing and baking.

Per cookie: 77 cal., 3 g total fat (2 g sat. fat), 9 mg chol., 37 mg sodium, 12 g carbo., 0 g fiber, 0 g pro.

Key Lime Cheesecake Bars

If you love the combination of sweet, salty and sour, this simple and quick-to-fix dessert has it all: a buttery pretzel-based crust and a lime-infused cheesecake-style filling topped with a sprinkling of roasted, salted pistachio nuts.

PREP: 20 minutes
BAKE: 350° for 30 to 35 minutes
COOL: 30 minutes
CHILL: 4 to 24 hours
MAKES: 15 to 20 bars

Crust:
- 1 **cup finely crushed pretzel sticks**
- 2 **tablespoons granulated sugar**
- ½ **cup (1 stick) butter, melted**

Filling:
- 2 **packages (8 ounces each) cream cheese, softened**
- ⅔ **cup granulated sugar**
- 1 **teaspoon vanilla extract**
- 3 **eggs, lightly beaten**
- 3 **tablespoons bottled key lime juice or regular lime juice**
- ½ **teaspoon finely shredded lime peel**
- ¼ **cup chopped, salted pistachio nuts**

1. Crust: Heat oven to 350°. Line 9×9×2-inch baking pan with foil, leaving about 1 inch of foil extending over the ends of the pan. Lightly grease foil; set pan aside.

2. In medium-size bowl, combine pretzels, the 2 tablespoons sugar and melted butter. Press mixture evenly in bottom of the prepared baking pan. Bake at 350° for 10 minutes. Cool on a wire rack while preparing filling.

3. Filling: In large mixing bowl, beat cream cheese, the ⅔ cup sugar and vanilla with electric mixer on medium speed until combined. Stir in eggs. Stir in lime juice and lime peel. Pour filling evenly over crust. Sprinkle with pistachio nuts.

4. Bake at 350° for 20 to 25 minutes or until center appears set. Cool in pan on a wire rack for 30 minutes. Cover and refrigerate for at least 4 hours or up to 24 hours (top will crack slightly). Remove bars from pan, using the foil to lift bars. Cut into bars.

Per bar: 254 cal., 19 g total fat (11 g sat. fat), 92 mg chol., 276 mg sodium, 17 g carbo., 0 g fiber, 4 g pro.

Malted Fudge Brownies

To toast the walnuts, spread them out in a single layer on a baking sheet. Bake in a 350° oven for 7 to 9 minutes, stirring once. Nuts burn very quickly, so check on them frequently. Let cool before using.

PREP: 40 minutes
BAKE: at 325° for 35 minutes
MAKES: 30 bars

1½ cups all-purpose flour
⅓ cup malted milk powder
½ teaspoon salt
1 cup (2 sticks) butter
4 ounces unsweetened chocolate, cut up
2 cups granulated sugar
4 eggs
1 teaspoon vanilla extract
1 cup chopped walnuts, toasted
4 ounces malted milk balls, coarsely crushed (about 1 cup)
½ of a can (15 to 16 ounces) chocolate fudge frosting

1. Heat oven to 325°. Lightly grease 13×9×2-inch baking pan; set aside. In medium-size bowl, combine flour, malted milk powder and salt; set aside.

2. In medium-size saucepan, melt butter and chocolate over low heat, stirring occasionally. Remove from heat; stir in granulated sugar. Beat in eggs, one at a time, with a wooden spoon. Add vanilla. Stir in flour mixture, walnuts and half of the malted milk balls. Spread in prepared pan.

3. Bake at 325° for 35 minutes. Cool in pan on a wire rack. Spread cooled brownies with frosting and sprinkle with remaining malted milk balls. Cut into bars.

Per bar: 245 cal., 14 g total fat (5 g sat. fat), 47 mg chol., 140 mg sodium, 29 g carbo., 1 g fiber, 3 g pro.

Pecan Pie Bars

These luscious bars have all of the rich flavor and nutty texture of classic pecan pie with a lot less work and mess and in much less time. Serve them with a pot of fresh-brewed coffee.

PREP: 25 minutes
BAKE: at 350° for 45 to 50 minutes
MAKES: 20 to 32 bars

2 cups all-purpose flour
½ cup granulated sugar
⅛ teaspoon salt
¾ cup (1½ sticks) butter
1 cup packed brown sugar
1 cup light-colored corn syrup
½ cup (1 stick) butter
4 eggs, lightly beaten
2½ cups finely chopped pecans
1 teaspoon vanilla extract

1. Heat oven to 350°. Grease 13×9×2-inch baking pan; set aside. In large bowl, stir together flour, granulated sugar and salt. With pastry blender, cut in the ¾ cup butter until mixture resembles fine crumbs. Press mixture evenly into prepared pan. Bake at 350° for 15 to 18 minutes or until lightly browned; set aside.

2. In medium-size saucepan, combine brown sugar, corn syrup and the ½ cup butter. Bring to a boil over medium heat, stirring constantly. Remove from heat. Place the eggs in medium-size bowl. Gradually stir about ½ cup of the hot mixture into the eggs. Return all mixture to saucepan. Stir in pecans and vanilla. Pour nut mixture over baked crust.

3. Bake at 350° for 30 to 32 minutes more or until filling is set. Cool in pan on a wire rack. Cut into bars.

Per bar: 343 cal., 22 g total fat (8 g sat. fat), 73 mg chol., 119 mg sodium, 34 g carbo., 2 g fiber, 4 g pro.

Dutch Almond Cherry-Filled Braids

With a few simple ingredients, a pair of kitchen shears, and a few well-paced snips, you can make a beautiful European-style pastry that looks and tastes like it came from the best bakery in town.

PREP: 30 minutes
STAND: 20 minutes
BAKE: at 375° for 30 to 35 minutes per braid
COOL: 15 minutes
MAKES: 2 braids (6 servings each)

- 1 **package (17.3 ounces) frozen puff pastry, thawed (2 sheets)**
- 1 **can (8 ounces) almond paste**
- ¼ **cup granulated sugar**
- 1 **egg, separated**
- ½ **cup cherry or raspberry preserves**
- 1 **tablespoon water**
- ¼ **cup sliced almonds**
  Coarse sugar

1. Heat oven to 375°. Line 2 large baking sheets with parchment paper. Unfold pastry sheets; place 1 pastry sheet on each prepared baking sheet.

2. In medium-size mixing bowl, beat almond paste, granulated sugar and egg white with electric mixer on medium speed until combined. Divide almond mixture between pastry sheets. Spread mixture over the center of each sheet in a 3-inch-wide strip, leaving a ½-inch border on each end. Spread preserves over almond filling.

3. With kitchen shears or sharp knife, make cuts at 1-inch intervals toward the filling about 3 inches long. Starting at one end, alternately fold opposite strips of dough at an angle across the filling, overlapping ends of strips in middle. Press down gently to seal.

4. Beat egg yolk with the water. Brush over braids. Sprinkle with almonds and coarse sugar. Cover lightly with plastic wrap and let stand for 20 minutes. Remove and discard plastic wrap.

5. Bake, one braid at a time, at 375° for 30 to 35 minutes or until tops and bottoms are golden brown. Cool braids on a wire rack about 15 minutes. Cut each braid into 6 slices; serve warm.

Per serving: 344 cal., 20 g total fat (1 g sat. fat), 18 mg chol., 165 mg sodium, 38 g carbo., 1 g fiber, 5 g pro.

Saucy Apple Dumplings

An apple corer—the kind that is shaped like a tube—makes quick work of readying these apples for baking. It's useful for making stuffed baked apples, too, and anytime you want to core an apple but leave it whole.

PREP: 30 minutes
BAKE: at 375° for 30 to 35 minutes
MAKES: 4 servings

- ½ package (17.3 ounces) frozen puff pastry (1 sheet), thawed
- 4 medium Granny Smith apples
- 1 tablespoon granulated sugar
- ½ teaspoon ground cinnamon
- 1 egg
- 1 teaspoon water
- ½ cup caramel ice-cream topping
- ⅓ cup chopped pecans, toasted

1. Unfold puff pastry on lightly floured surface. Roll pastry into 14-inch square. With knife, cut pastry into four 7-inch squares. Set aside.

2. Heat oven to 375°. Peel and core the apples. If necessary, trim bottoms of the apples so they stand upright. Place an apple in the center of each pastry square. In small bowl, combine granulated sugar and cinnamon; spoon into centers of the apples.

3. In another small bowl, beat egg and the water with fork. Moisten the edges of the pastry squares with egg mixture; fold corners to center over fruit. Pinch to seal, pleating and folding pastry along seams as necessary. Place dumplings in 13×9×2-inch baking pan. Brush wrapped apples with egg mixture.

4. Bake, uncovered, at 375° for 30 to 35 minutes or until fruit is tender and pastry is golden.

5. In microwave-safe 2-cup glass measuring cup, combine ice-cream topping and pecans; microwave, uncovered, on 100% power (high) for 30 to 60 seconds or until heated through.

6. Serve dumplings warm with pecan mixture.

Per serving: 567 cal., 28 g total fat (1 g sat. fat), 53 mg chol., 362 mg sodium, 77 g carbo., 5 g fiber, 5 g pro.

Apple Dumplings with Cranberry-Sour Cream Filling: Prepare apples as directed at left, except omit sugar and cinnamon filling mixture. In small bowl, combine 2 tablespoons sour cream, 2 tablespoons packed brown sugar, 2 tablespoons dried cranberries, 2 tablespoons chopped toasted pecans or walnuts and, if desired, ½ teaspoon finely shredded orange peel. Fill apple centers with sour cream mixture. Continue as directed.

Apple Dumplings with Raisin-Walnut Filling: Prepare apples as directed at left, except omit sugar and cinnamon filling. For raisin-walnut filling, in small bowl, combine 2 tablespoons chopped raisins, 2 tablespoons chopped walnuts and 1 tablespoon honey. Fill apples with raisin-walnut filling; sprinkle with a mixture of 1 teaspoon granulated sugar and ⅛ teaspoon ground cinnamon. Divide 1 tablespoon butter between the apples, placing on top of filling. Continue as directed.

Cinnamon Swirl Bread Pudding

Balsamic vinegar as a dessert ingredient isn't as odd as it might seem at first blush. It adds its characteristically rich brown color and caramelly flavor to a cinnamon-spiced sauce for drizzling atop this warm bread pudding.

PREP: 35 minutes
BAKE: at 350° for 1 hour
COOL: 30 minutes
MAKES: 12 servings

Bread Pudding:
- 1 loaf (1 pound) cinnamon-swirl raisin bread, cut into ½-inch cubes
- 1 cup slivered almonds, toasted
- ½ cup snipped dried apricots
- 3 eggs, lightly beaten
- 4 cups milk
- 1¼ cups granulated sugar
- 1 teaspoon vanilla extract
- ½ teaspoon almond extract

Balsamic-Cinnamon Sauce:
- ¼ cup packed brown sugar
- 2 tablespoons (¼ stick) butter
- 2 tablespoons balsamic vinegar
- ¼ teaspoon ground cinnamon

1. Bread Pudding: Heat oven to 350°. Grease 13×9×2-inch baking dish; set aside. In very large bowl, combine bread cubes, almonds and apricots; set aside.

2. In large bowl, stir together eggs, milk, granulated sugar, vanilla extract and almond extract. Stir egg mixture into bread mixture. Pour in prepared dish.

3. Bake, covered with foil, at 350° for 45 minutes. Remove foil; bake at 350° about 15 minutes more or until puffed and a knife inserted near the center comes out clean. Cool about 30 minutes.

4. Balsamic-Cinnamon Sauce: In small saucepan, combine brown sugar, butter, balsamic vinegar and cinnamon. Cook and stir until mixture comes to a boil. Serve warm sauce over warm bread pudding.

Per serving: 354 cal., 10 g total fat (4 g sat. fat), 70 mg chol., 221 mg sodium, 56 g carbo., 3 g fiber, 10 g pro.

Rhubarb Surprise Crisp

The "surprise" in this otherwise old-fashioned dessert is a sprinkling of fresh basil. Although it may sound odd, try it! Basil's licorice-like flavor is a wonderful complement to the flavor of the fruit.

PREP: 20 minutes
BAKE: at 375° for 30 to 35 minutes
COOL: 20 minutes
MAKES: 6 servings

- ⅔ cup granulated sugar
- 2 or 3 teaspoons cornstarch
- ¼ teaspoon ground cinnamon
- 2 cups sliced fresh rhubarb or frozen unsweetened sliced rhubarb, thawed
- 2 cups coarsely chopped fresh strawberries
- 2 tablespoons chopped fresh basil leaves
- ½ cup all-purpose flour
- ½ cup quick-cooking rolled oats
- ⅓ cup packed brown sugar
- ¼ teaspoon salt
- 3 tablespoons butter, melted
  Sweetened whipped cream, for serving (optional)

1. Heat oven to 375°. In medium-size bowl, combine granulated sugar, cornstarch and cinnamon. (For fresh rhubarb, use 2 teaspoons cornstarch. For frozen, use 3 teaspoons cornstarch.) Stir in rhubarb, strawberries and basil. Spoon into 8×8×2-inch baking dish, spreading evenly; set aside.

2. In another medium-size bowl, combine flour, oats, brown sugar and salt. Stir in melted butter. Sprinkle over fruit.

3. Bake at 375° for 30 to 35 minutes or until fruit is tender and topping is golden brown. Serve warm. If desired, top with sweetened whipped cream.

Per serving: 281 cal., 7 g total fat (4 g sat. fat), 15 mg chol., 144 mg sodium, 54 g carbo., 3 g fiber, 3 g pro.

Peanut Butter Cupcakes

There's a surprise inside each of these PB&J cupcakes—a bite-size peanut butter cup. (So you get to have your cupcake and a little bit of candy, too.)

PREP: 45 minutes
BAKE: at 350° about 18 minutes
COOL: 20 minutes
MAKES: 24 cupcakes

- 1⅓ cups all-purpose flour
- ⅔ cup graham cracker crumbs
- 1 tablespoon baking powder
- 1 cup creamy peanut butter
- ⅓ cup solid vegetable shortening
- 1⅓ cups granulated sugar
- 2 eggs
- 1 teaspoon vanilla extract
- 1 cup milk
- 24 bite-size chocolate-covered peanut butter cups
  Raspberry or strawberry jam

1. Heat oven to 350°. Line 24 cups of standard-size muffin pans with paper bake cups; set aside. In medium-size bowl, stir together flour, graham cracker crumbs and baking powder; set aside.

2. In very large mixing bowl, beat peanut butter and shortening with electric mixer on medium speed until combined. Gradually add granulated sugar, beating on medium speed, until well combined. Beat in eggs and vanilla. Alternately add flour mixture and milk to peanut butter mixture, beating on low speed after each addition just until combined.

3. Spoon a rounded tablespoon of batter into each prepared muffin cup. Unwrap peanut butter cups and place one in each muffin cup on top of the batter. Spoon remaining batter into muffin cups to cover peanut butter cups. Bake at 350° about 18 minutes or until wooden toothpick inserted near edges comes out clean (cupcakes may have a slight indentation). Cool cupcakes in muffin cups on wire racks for 5 minutes. Remove cupcakes from muffin cups; cool thoroughly on wire racks. Spoon a small amount of jam on top of each cupcake.

Per cupcake: 295 cal., 15 g total fat (5 g sat. fat), 21 mg chol., 139 mg sodium, 38 g carbo., 2 g fiber, 6 g pro.

Butterscotch Crunch Squares

This frozen ice cream dessert has a top and bottom crumb crust of oats, brown sugar, butter and nuts. It's creamy and crunchy in one bite!

PREP: 40 minutes
BAKE: at 400° for 10 to 15 minutes
COOL: 30 minutes
FREEZE: 6 hours
STAND: 5 to 10 minutes
MAKES: 12 squares

- 1 cup all-purpose flour
- ¼ cup quick-cooking rolled oats
- ¼ cup packed brown sugar
- ½ cup (1 stick) butter
- ½ cup chopped pecans or walnuts
- ½ cup butterscotch-flavored or caramel-flavored ice cream topping
- ½ gallon butter-brickle, chocolate or vanilla ice cream

1. Heat oven to 400°. In medium-size bowl, combine flour, oats and brown sugar. With pastry blender, cut in butter until mixture resembles coarse crumbs. Stir in nuts. Pat mixture lightly into ungreased 13×9×2-inch baking pan. Bake at 400° for 10 to 15 minutes. Remove from oven. While still warm, stir nut mixture to crumble. Cool completely.

2. Spread half of the crumbs in 9×9×2-inch pan; drizzle about half of the ice-cream topping over crumbs in pan. Place ice cream in chilled medium-size bowl; stir to soften. Spoon softened ice cream carefully over topping-drizzled crumbs. Drizzle with remaining topping; sprinkle with the remaining crumbs. Cover and freeze at least 6 hours or until firm. Let stand at room temperature for 5 to 10 minutes before serving.

Per square: 450 cal., 28 g total fat (15 g sat. fat), 112 mg chol., 156 mg sodium, 46 g carbo., 1 g fiber, 5 g pro.

Chocolate-Raspberry Cheesecake

For the creamiest, crack-free cheesecake, take it from the oven when a 2½-inch area around the edge of the cake appears set. Don't worry if the center looks fairly loose—it will firm up as the cheesecake cools.

PREP: 40 minutes
BAKE: at 350° for 50 to 60 minutes
COOL: 1¾ hours
CHILL: 4 hours
MAKES: 16 servings

Crust:
- 1½ **cups finely crushed graham crackers**
- ¼ **cup confectioners' sugar**
- ⅓ **cup butter, melted**

Filling:
- 2 **cups fresh or frozen raspberries, thawed**
- ½ **teaspoon granulated sugar**
- 3 **packages (8 ounces each) cream cheese, softened**
- 1 **can (14 ounces) sweetened condensed milk (1¼ cups)**
- 4 **eggs**
- 1 **teaspoon vanilla extract**
- 1 **cup semisweet chocolate chips (6 ounces), melted and cooled**
- **Chocolate curls (optional)**

1. Crust: Heat oven to 350°. In small bowl, combine crushed graham crackers and confectioners' sugar; stir in melted butter. Press onto bottom and about 2 inches up the sides of a 9-inch springform pan; set aside.

2. Filling: In small bowl, combine 1 cup of the raspberries and the granulated sugar; set aside. In large mixing bowl, beat cream cheese and sweetened condensed milk with electric mixer on low speed until combined. Add eggs and vanilla; beat just until combined. Divide batter in half. Stir melted chocolate into half of the batter. Pour chocolate batter into the crust-lined pan. Stir raspberry-sugar mixture into remaining batter. Spoon raspberry batter over chocolate batter.

3. Place springform pan in a shallow baking pan. Bake at 350° for 50 to 60 minutes or until a 2½-inch area around the edge appears set when gently shaken.

4. Cool in pan on a wire rack for 15 minutes. Using a small knife, loosen crust from pan sides. Cool for 30 minutes. Remove side of pan; cool completely on wire rack. Cover; refrigerate for at least 4 hours before serving. Serve with remaining raspberries and chocolate curls, if desired.

Per serving: 387 cal., 26 g total fat (16 g sat. fat), 118 mg chol., 278 mg sodium, 32 g carbo., 2 g fiber, 8 g pro.

Index

Note: Boldfaced page references indicate photographs.

Note: Boldfaced page references indicate photographs.

Note: Boldfaced page references indicate photographs.

Metric Information

The charts on this page provide a guide for converting measurements from the U.S. customary system, which is used throughout this book, to the metric system.

PRODUCT DIFFERENCES

Most of the ingredients called for in the recipes in this book are available in most countries. However, some are known by different names. Here are some common American ingredients and their possible counterparts:

■ Sugar (white) is granulated, fine granulated, or castor sugar.

■ Confectioners' sugar is icing sugar.

■ All-purpose flour is enriched, bleached, or unbleached white household flour. When self-rising flour is used in place of all-purpose flour in a recipe that calls for leavening, omit the leavening agent (baking soda or baking powder) and salt.

■ Light-colored corn syrup is golden syrup.

■ Cornstarch is cornflour.

■ Baking soda is bicarbonate of soda.

■ Vanilla or vanilla extract is vanilla essence.

■ Green, red, or yellow sweet peppers are capsicums or bell peppers.

■ Golden raisins are sultanas.

VOLUME AND WEIGHT

The United States traditionally uses cup measures for liquid and solid ingredients. The chart, top right, shows the approximate imperial and metric equivalents. If you are accustomed to weighing solid ingredients, the following approximate equivalents will be helpful.

■ 1 cup butter, castor sugar, or rice = 8 ounces = 1/2 pound = 250 grams

■ 1 cup flour = 4 ounces = 1/4 pound = 125 grams

■ 1 cup icing sugar = 5 ounces = 150 grams

Canadian and U.S. volume for a cup measure is 8 fluid ounces (237 ml), but the standard metric equivalent is 250 ml.

1 British imperial cup is 10 fluid ounces.

In Australia, 1 tablespoon equals 20 ml, and there are 4 teaspoons in the Australian tablespoon.

Spoon measures are used for smaller amounts of ingredients. Although the size of the tablespoon varies slightly in different countries, for practical purposes and for recipes in this book, a straight substitution is all that's necessary. Measurements made using cups or spoons always should be level unless stated otherwise.

COMMON WEIGHT RANGE REPLACEMENTS

Imperial / U.S.	Metric
1/2 ounce	15 g
1 ounce	25 g or 30 g
4 ounces (1/4 pound)	115 g or 125 g
8 ounces (1/2 pound)	225 g or 250 g
16 ounces (1 pound)	450 g or 500 g
1 1/4 pounds	625 g
1 1/2 pounds	750 g
2 pounds or 2 1/4 pounds	1,000 g or 1 Kg

OVEN TEMPERATURE EQUIVALENTS

Fahrenheit Setting	Celsius Setting*	Gas Setting
300°F	150°C	Gas Mark 2 (very low)
325°F	160°C	Gas Mark 3 (low)
350°F	180°C	Gas Mark 4 (moderate)
375°F	190°C	Gas Mark 5 (moderate)
400°F	200°C	Gas Mark 6 (hot)
425°F	220°C	Gas Mark 7 (hot)
450°F	230°C	Gas Mark 8 (very hot)
475°F	240°C	Gas Mark 9 (very hot)
500°F	260°C	Gas Mark 10 (extremely hot)
Broil	Broil	Grill

*Electric and gas ovens may be calibrated using celsius. However, for an electric oven, increase celsius setting 10 to 20 degrees when cooking above 160°C. For convection or forced air ovens (gas or electric) lower the temperature setting 25°F/10°C when cooking at all heat levels.

BAKING PAN SIZES

Imperial / U.S.	Metric
9×1 1/2-inch round cake pan	22- or 23×4-cm (1.5 L)
9×1 1/2-inch pie plate	22- or 23×4-cm (1 L)
8×8×2-inch square cake pan	20×5-cm (2 L)
9×9×2-inch square cake pan	22- or 23×4.5-cm (2.5 L)
11×7×1 1/2-inch baking pan	28×17×4-cm (2 L)
2-quart rectangular baking pan	30×19×4.5-cm (3 L)
13×9×2-inch baking pan	34×22×4.5-cm (3.5 L)
15×10×1-inch jelly roll pan	40×25×2-cm
9×5×3-inch loaf pan	23×13×8-cm (2 L)
2-quart casserole	2 L

U.S. / STANDARD METRIC EQUIVALENTS

1/8 teaspoon = 0.5 ml	1/3 cup = 3 fluid ounces = 75 ml
1/4 teaspoon = 1 ml	1/2 cup = 4 fluid ounces = 125 ml
1/2 teaspoon = 2 ml	1/3 cup = 5 fluid ounces = 150 ml
1 teaspoon = 5 ml	3/4 cup = 6 fluid ounces = 175 ml
1 tablespoon = 15 ml	1 cup = 8 fluid ounces = 250 ml
2 tablespoons = 25 ml	2 cups = 1 pint = 500 ml
1/4 cup = 2 fluid ounces = 50 ml	1 quart = 1 litre